THERE'S ALWAYS ONE

10 Years of Watching Northern Ireland
June 1995 – June 2005

SHAUN SCHOFIELD

DIABLE VERT
PUBLICATIONS

First published in 2006 by
Diable Vert Publications, Gt. Britain.

This edition published 2006 by
Diable Vert Publications,
PO Box 4292, Dunstable,
Bedfordshire LU6 9AR.

Schofield, Shaun 1966-.

There's Always One:
Ten Years of Watching Northern Ireland

ISBN 0-9552101-0-0
ISBN 978-0-9552101-0-5

Printed in Gt. Britain by Styletype Printing.

Dedicated to my Mum and Dad and to any supporter of Northern Ireland, wherever you are!

ACKNOWLEDGEMENTS

I would like to thank the following people for their help and support in physically publishing this work.

The officers of the Irish Football Association who have supported this venture.

Roy Bennett who put me in touch with Davey Watt from Styletype Printing, who in turn generously printed this publication at no profit.

Marshall Gillespie, who burnt many an hour of midnight oil in proofing and editing this book.

Finally, to my partner Rebecca, whose computing skills have made my written words on bits of paper, a saleable reality.

IRISH
FOOTBALL
ASSOCIATION

Dear Shaun,

In my time as Manager the 'Green and White Army' has grown in almost biblical proportions. To take 5500 supporters to the Millennium Stadium or 6500 to Old Trafford is quite an achievement even if they are only 'over the water'. But for the team to come out in Azerbaijan and find over 100 of the G&W Army was amazing! And the 1600 who went to Austria is the largest travelling support NI have taken in mainland Europe since 1982.

A special mention to Shaun who has followed us home and away for the last 10 years, definitely well beyond the call of duty!

It was great that I was able to address the G & W Army personally after the game in Austria. The announcer came over to me and asked "What are they all still doing here? The game is over." "What they are doing" I replied "Is enjoying being the best fans in the world"

Onwards and Upwards,

Lawrie Sanchez

20 Windsor Avenue
Belfast BT9 6EE

Telephone:
028 9066 9458

Facsimile:
028 9066 7620

E-mail:
enquiries@irishfa.com

Web:
www.irishfa.com

Daily Mirror sponsored
Virtual Message Board
09062 111112

HOUSE OF COMMONS
LONDON SW1A 0AA

Any football supporter who manages to attend all the matches home and away of their country is worthy of acclaim. Shaun Schofield has followed Northern Ireland for 10 years without missing a single match. What makes this even more remarkable is that Shaun is not from Northern Ireland, but from England and yet he has become arguably the most ardent 'green and white' army fan living anywhere.

I have met Shaun when he is travelling abroad to a Northern Ireland match and he represents all the very best in a football supporter. Northern Ireland has undoubtedly the best supporters amongst the Home Countries. Not only do they behave impeccably but their singing and support for the team, even when losing, is legendary.

Travelling supporters are great ambassadors for their country and it is because of people like Shaun that all over the world there are people who have never visited Northern Ireland and who are never likely to, but who have been left with a warm regard for 'our wee country' and its people.

I wish the book every success.

Kate HoeyMP Vauxhall and former Sports Minister

FOREWORD

"Northern Ireland is very fortunate to have many tremendous supporters who follow their team both at home and abroad.

Shaun Schofield started following Northern Ireland in 1995 and during that time has never missed a match that Northern Ireland has been involved in. I have known Shaun during most of this period and he has been a tremendous supporter not only to me but also to the Irish Football Association. Ironically Shaun is not a born and bred Ulsterman but he fell in love with 'Our Wee Country' as it is described by many of our journalists and certainly can claim to be their Number 1 fan. On away trips Shaun has not seen the team win too many games, but has always had a very pleasant manner and has been a great ambassador for his adopted country and has made many friendships amongst the Northern Ireland supporters.

I would like to wish Shaun every success with the venture that he has undertaken. It is typical of Shaun that he does not wish to make any financial gain for himself and I am sure the charities will be very grateful for the money that he is donating from the proceeds of this book. I hope that many Northern Irish people buy this wonderful book as Shaun deserves all the support that he can get".

Best Wishes

Jim Boyce
President: Irish Football Association

PROLOGUE

When Northern Ireland played Germany on June 4th 2005, it was not only the Irish Football Association (IFA) who was celebrating an anniversary. They were acknowledging 125 years of soccer administration in the island of Ireland, and latterly, since 1921 in the six counties recognised as Northern Ireland. Football politics and tradition is murky in Ireland, but the nation of Eire unilaterally set up their association when the state of Ireland was founded: hence their title; Football Association of Ireland (FAI).

Though I have been watching Northern Ireland play regularly since September 1994, the June celebration was a reason for personal triumph, in that a decade had passed since I missed a fixture. Work commitments and a need to relocate caused my absence from the 1995 Canada tour, which took in fixtures against Chile and the host nation.

Of course, other supporters have not missed a home game for many a year and express genuine pride at being inside Windsor Park, when so many thousand watched the so-called 'glory nights' as (Northern) Ireland qualified for World Cup finals in 1958, 1982 and 1986. Similarly, groups of supporters, most especially members of the 1st Shankill Northern Ireland Supporters' Club, tell of the abject misery of visiting Ceauceascu's Romania in the 1980s, or Bulgarian hotels bereft of food. However, I do believe, save for IFA luminaries such as chef de partie Derek McKinley, and the doyen of Ulster sports journalism, Malcolm Brodie, who incidentally, has not missed a World Cup since World War II, that I am the only person who has attended every match.

Moreover, since June 7th 1995, when this journey began, I have paid to attend every one of the 78 matches. In 'non-accountancy' estimates, the cost for travel, hotels and tickets is probably approaching £25,000: exclusive of drunken parties, one-night stands, trips to capital city viewing towers, coach trips to the River Kwai, and visits to football 'spectaculars', including the 1998 World Cup Finals, and various UEFA Finals. In accountant talk, this is £7 a day habit: equal to setting 30 cigarettes on fire daily or drinking 2.5 extra pints a day on the way home. Health wise therefore it is good value, although watching Northern Ireland at times is not for the faint hearted, but it would have been a great down payment as a mortgage.

The latter is something I do not have, and I am very pro-European in that thinking. Personally, I am prepared always to rent a roof over my head, as I can see little benefit in saving groomed piles of bricks. That view may be different if I had commitments, but I am single, have no children and in a selfish mode, do not see myself as having to provide for anyone save myself. Hence my spending habits.

The Northern Ireland journey actually started in February 1993, when I joined the team charter to Albania: then Europe's poorest nation, but previously Europe's most hermit-like nation. This was the reason for undertaking the trip, because my upper-form school geography teacher, Dennis Child once said 'Albania is a funny country, a Stalinist state, non-aligned to anyone (USSR or The West) and they do not speak to anyone'. That phrase seemed to stick and I just wanted to satisfy my curiosity, which had festered when I read little snippets about life in Albania or seen an occasional football international from Tirana: one such when Albania beat Spain 2-0 in the mid 80s. I guess Enver Hoxha, the undisputed leader, he who shot his Foreign Minister at a Cabinet meeting, must have stressed his communist ideals and his collective paradise on his subjects to an even greater extent after that day in history.

I could not even attempt to explain why this comment stuck in my mind, but the experiences I have had following Northern Ireland, initially ten years after Albania was first impressed on me would suggest I am glad it did.

I have to say that apart from Russell Buckroyd, who had free licence to bully and abuse, bearing in mind he was the deputy headmaster's son, my school days were generally happy ones. Indeed, I spent a decade at King Edward VII School by the seaside in Lytham St.Annes, near Blackpool. I was never the brightest student, but always made what I felt was a justifiable academic effort, especially since Dad paid fees for me and my younger sister to attend the best local schools. Sure, I skimped on school dinners, which Dad knew about as I found out in later years, got into the odd situation or three with Carl Simmons, and had heated exchanges with numerous teachers, but I left with 8 O-Levels and 4 A-Levels.

Our teachers, Dennis Child included, always promoted students keeping abreast of current affairs. Indeed, PE cum geography master, Alan Jones, even advocated us watching the weather on television when studying climate for O-Level. This was no problem, as Dad was a family businessman, principally involved in newspapers, and the news was important to him, particularly in strife-torn seventies Britain, when printers, journalists, railway workers and transporters sought, not personally, though it seemed that way in our lounge, to damage his livelihood. (For the record, the weather was also viewed with a hard intensity given my father's golfing hobby or the family thirst for summer picnics). Northern Ireland; 'the province', 'the troubles', Catholics, Protestants, H-Blocks and assorted bombs and shootings, particularly in Belfast, Londonderry, and bizarrely, Crossmaglen also always seemed to occupy a prominence on the teatime news bulletins of the seventies. It was difficult to comprehend these words and places with the absolute peace and innocence of my childhood, but I also always wondered what this part of Great Britain was really like. One vision of normality, save on occasional Nationwide evening programme extolling the virtues of the beauty of the Antrim coast, was via the now defunct British Home International Football Championships, which except for the England v Scotland fixture, was a highlighted package of football. From the late seventies, when I began to take a memory lasting interest in football this was an annual chance to see a part of 'normal' Belfast due to a football match or two from Windsor Park, complete with the odd corner flags, with LFC embossed in blue. (I later found out they were to signify Linfield Football Club, the landlords of Windsor Park). For some reason, I had a slight hankering for the underdog, which was always Northern Ireland against England, and, though I wanted England to win, Northern Ireland came a close second. Indeed, I was more than happy to lend my tele-visual 'support' to Northern Ireland at the World Cup in Spain in 1982. That story belongs in other books, as does the team exploits of 1986 in Mexico. I will mention though how delighted I was, in Mum's best lounge in front of a steam driven black and white television, on that Friday night in June when 'Arcanada.... Armstrong' said John Motson, as Gerry Armstrong netted the winner against the hosts.

Turning the clock forward now to September 1994, a first visit to Northern Ireland eventually occurred, via the insistence of Gavin Nixon, whom I met in Albania and is perhaps therefore the whole reason for my 10 year journey, more of which will be explained in due course. I felt both odd and misinformed on that first visit. Odd that I had travelled to many places in the world, including the USA (twice), a dark and grey Poland, 15 months after the collapse of the Berlin Wall, and Albania, and yet had not given a part of my own country a chance, prior to this date, to extol its worth: misinformed (and angry) in that people lived a 'normal' life, spending the same currency in the same shops, went to the same offices and carried out the same hobbies, rather than running some kind of highway man operation on Dodge-City street corners and having gelignite in their briefcases; as some of the media would have you believe. Given that small towns had traffic barriers to prevent car bombs and the police drove around in armour plated Land Rovers, I was not naïve enough to realise some of that previously explained did not go on, but the sheer scale of normality genuinely surprised me. This first visit was one week after the Provisional IRA announced their initial ceasefire and whether it was due to this, or not, I was amazed, and still am, by the warmth of the inhabitants of Ulster who always want to know your business and seem to welcome you with open arms; be they football supporters, shoppers returning to the Bogside in Londonderry or market traders in Antrim. This is an important part of my returning these past years. Occasionally, I have thought that the football has become secondary on occasions, and the social side of visiting Belfast more primary; particularly as I now visit for friends' weddings and even for drinking weekends to celebrate the fact that the 3rd Carrickfergus Silver Band merely exists.

The word 'friend' is one I often struggle with, because I wonder who exactly should be defined as a friend, and often conclude that they should be considered as someone whom would not shout at you if you knock on their door, destitute at 3 am. in the morning, but would greet you with phrase 'Come in!'. Those are few and far between and can normally be counted on one hand and personally incorporate my parents, my brother Ben, whom I have leant on like most family siblings do from time to time, and Keith and Sarah Pollitt, who have fed, housed and employed me, when my heart has ruled my head in personal circumstances when I have told employers what I think of them. I also consider David and Tracey Charlut in Calais as friends, as they willingly helped me out when I was struggling with the legions of French civil servants, who I decided on occasions were only there to conspire against me personally. However, for purposes below, I will use the looser, more accepted term, in that friends are people you can have a drink, a laugh and spend time with. Perhaps 'mates' is a better term of phrase.

Though they may not know it, some of those friends and acquaintances have simply made it possible for me to keep watching Northern Ireland and I would like to thank the following people and organisations in no particular order.

Initially, to the staff and luminaries of Irish Football Association whom I have pestered for ticket and travel information over the years and in particular Lesley Russell (nee Brown) who relentlessly answers the switchboard phone, David Currie and Glenda Dines and the office staff who have furnished me with match tickets for many games, despite the incompetence of the French postal service. Also to President Jim Boyce, who allowed me to attend the match in Armenia in 1997, via a team charter, in the days when distance air travel was a luxury enjoyed by the few.

My thanks to Gavin Nixon, who initially suggested I buy a season ticket for games at Windsor Park, who along with John Aiken has saved me a small fortune in hotel bills in Northern Ireland by offering spare bedrooms, as well as complimentary catering facilities. Though they will not know it, my gratitude goes also to the various hotels around the world who have had to clean green paint smeared sheets and bathrooms after my visits, as well as airlines, especially Easyjet, whose founding has saved me at least £100 a trip on 'home' games in Belfast. A 1994 trip to Belfast from Birmingham cost me £151, yet a 2004 midweek overnight trip comes in at only £40.

Thank you also to travelling companions, Gavin and John, occasional excursionists Gavin Lavery and Robert Hunter, who saved me from a personal abyss in Kiev in 1997, and 'regular' Robert Walsh with whom I have travelled since 2001 and shared many expenses, sore heads and lumpy beds in Eastern Europe.

A final compliment must also be offered to my employers and workmates over the last fifteen years who allowed me to have 'difficult' days off and changed their shifts for me to attend football matches. I have quoted fifteen years here, as I began travelling to international football in 1990, have attended some 200 internationals, none of which incorporate a two week package holiday or a week off at Christmas, but Saturdays away from leisure operations and days away from midweek operational meetings. Sure I have signed my holiday requests, but in the main, save for the likes of occasional line-managers' personal enmity and jealousy, employers have supported what has, at times, become an obsession: some even commenting on the sadness they think I suffer when Northern Ireland have lost again. My most previous employer, Remarkable Restaurants, even allowed me a 10 day Caribbean Tour holiday in May 2004, with full blessing, only six weeks after taking up an appointment. I am never depressed or sad when Northern Ireland lose, as football is insignificant in terms of the dreadful suffering I have seen humans endure in this ten-year journey. I hope I will explain my emotions in supporting Northern Ireland, the stories and tales of the characters I have met and endured and my feelings in the world we share in the following pages.

Finally, I would like to mention that I have written this book entirely from memory and not used any notes or information sources save my own and intend that any proceeds from the sale of this book to go those more needy than myself.

THE OPPORTUNITY

Throughout all our personal experiences, most probably when the worse for alcohol in front of the television at Christmas, I guess we can all remember sitting with an in-law or an elderly family member who has, at some point, unilaterally boarded their personal memory lane and mentioned the onset of ITV, or colour movies or fast train travel. For me, it was my granddad, who had flown to Spain in the early 1970s on a package holiday to the winter sunshine. I guess this was the 'telephone' of the today, but as far as our family was concerned it was something that would pass us by.

It was a non-starter, because Dad ran his own business. Being a wholesale newsagent for the Southern Fylde Coast was a seven-day a week job and today, though long retired, he often reminisces about how he looked forward to Christmas Day, Boxing Day and Good Friday because there were no papers. This was akin to a "fortnight holiday package" and he and Mum always made sure the family had a good time on such days, and to a lesser extent during the picnic days of high summer with a trip to Chester Zoo. The only family holidays were a snatched couple of days at a conference in Eastbourne or Torquay.

In reflection, I always felt I missed a right of passage and I was 23 when I actually first got my feet off the ground. Indeed, it was only in 2002 that my father first flew. No short hop to Dublin either: a long haul to Johannesburg via Paris to see his sister. As for my mother, she is quite happy making swathes of homemade jam and doting over the grandchildren!

Fate takes peculiar twists, but in 1989 I was studying for a degree in Sports Studies at Roehampton Institute in South West London, and one of the guide booklets suggested under-graduates were encouraged to be spectators at 'live' sports events. No second request was required here and the student grant went on tickets for snooker, tennis, ice hockey, badminton, rugby at Twickenham, and football at Wembley. I had been to Wembley, like many schoolchildren in the 70s, to watch England play Scotland schoolboys on a school trip (for girls it was a trip to the Twin Towers to watch the national ladies' hockey team). Though a pleasant March day, I remembered Wembley as a cold, corrugated place with high fences and was most disappointed to see the roof made of off-green plastic tiling rather than the virginal white the television screen at home had shown when casting the F.A. Cup Final. On returning in November 1989, when England played Italy, it felt as if nothing had changed. Roof wise, it hadn't.

As far as I was concerned, international football always had a significant importance; because unlike today, when Rupert Murdoch's media enterprises show a dozen live games a week, the bleak growing up days brought only live football in the form of internationals involving England or the Cup Final, which, in itself was like a family programme with a special Question of Sport and walks up Wembley way with Jimmy Tarbuck. Occasionally, England's matches would involve playing behind the old Soviet Iron Curtain, meaning an afternoon kick-off to save on floodlight electric. As school finished at 3.30, very infrequently you may catch some of a game before children's programmes started at 4.00p.m. For me, the main features were that it was daytime television; a novelty in itself, a grainy whistling commentary and an occasional action reply from behind a goal, with a large flashing 'R' in the left hand corner signifying a replay. I last saw this, much to Gavin Nixon's amusement, when watching the Moldova v England game, from Chisnau in 1996, but with 70s technology it was a big innovation.

Watching a 'live' international brought these memories back and I simply developed a thirst for international football. I continued to visit Wembley during that winter and spring to watch England's build-up games to Italia '90; of which there were a number, because England appeared 'unofficially' banned from playing abroad, as clubs were suspended due to the Heysel disaster, and the F.A. were desperate to get this overturned. Also the Thatcher government did not want scenes of English supporters running amuck further splashed over the world's media, as it was considered a national embarrassment.

At this point, I feel I should point out that I did not, during formative years, and do not have a club team on which I spend money supporting. Dad's hobbies were breeding gun dogs, latterly replaced by golf and now a love of motorbikes, and rugby, which meant many Saturday afternoons watching Fylde. There was little football stock in the family and even today Dad uses some expletive coupled with 'overpaid', when describing footballers. (I can often see his point.) As such, and due to the fact we lived three miles from the nearest town and off a bus-route, and local teams Blackpool and Preston North End were very much on the slide in the late 70s, my interest in club football was marginal. This is compounded by the fact that since I fled the family nest in 1988, I have lived in twelve locations, including two addresses in France, and felt no real affinity to any of them or their respective football teams, save perhaps Kidderminster Harriers, who, in the 1990s were pushing for League status from Conference anonymity.

Therefore an England match gave me a sense of a supporter 'belonging', which I had missed without a club team and one I personally developed into other sports, especially cricket and rugby; though the latter has a sense of social occasion, but a meeting between any countries will do as far as I am concerned.

The end of a football season always culminated in the aforementioned Home International Championship (of which Northern Ireland are holders) until 1985, when England and Scotland dubiously went their own ways under the guise of finding better opposition to improve their competitive international fortunes. The spurious Rous Cup was developed, named after a famous English football diplomat, where England still played Scotland. However, Thatcher paranoia over hooliganism in the fountains of Trafalgar Square even killed that off, leaving England playing friendlies at Wembley, against the USSR and Uruguay prior to the 1990 World Cup.

Wembley programmes were always a complete rip-off, but without a programme, even if it was a bit of paper out of the press box in poverty stricken provincial Armenia, and my ticket stub, I feel I have not been to a sporting event. As such, I would shell out my £3 (even in 1990) for a few pictures, a welcome message from various Wembley and F.A. luminaries, and Wembley adverts suggesting a good night out was at the dog track on a Friday or watching some washed up musician like Gary Glitter or Mud mime a few Christmas hits. The Uruguay programme was different though, in that adverts were from travel companies offering day-trips to Sardinia to watch England play Holland in Italia '90. In short, the rest of summer term's local authority student grant went on such a trip.

England qualified for Italia '90 and were deemed, via its hooligan element, unsuitable to inhabit, initially at least, the boot of Italy and were banished to the outpost of Sardinia. Matters got worse for the authorities in December 1989, when at the draw for the World Cup Finals groups, Holland, who had a growing cancer of hooliganism following the national team, were paired with England (and the Republic of Ireland and Egypt). It appeared the idea was to closely monitor supporters on the island and 'fly-in/fly-out' as many supporters as possible, and have a total alcohol ban on match days in

Sardinia. Hence the 'one-day tour', in travel agent speak, was advertised.

The England v Holland (who were the present European Champions and had players such as Gullitt, Van Baasten and Rijkaard) game on 15th June 1990 was, as well as the first time I had flown anywhere, deemed as the tie which would determine who would progress from the group with an easier fixture in the last sixteen.

The atmosphere inside the ground 'hooked' me. It was the first 'competitive' game I had attended and I had decided even before the game started that more had to follow. I was high on atmosphere, incorporating the support, the authoritarian and scary Caribinieri and the game itself. For the record, the game finished 0-0, England had the better of it and controversy abounded when Stuart Pearce attempted an indirect free kick shot on goal. Whether a Dutch limb touched the ball on its way into Van Breukkelen's net, to given England victory, is a subject of debate even today.

My personal high collapsed some five hours later when I was taken to Caligari's hospital with lesions of the cornea. I had travelled to Italy wearing contact lenses and as I was a virgin flier, I had not realised aeroplane cabin airflow is stale and can dry tear ducts. The brutal summer sun and dusty atmosphere in Sardinia had not helped the situation and had ultimately led my eyes to clog with dust that a lack of tears could not dissipate. The conclusion - a night in hospital with my eyes taped and plastered shut.

For the first time in my life I was genuinely scared. Doctors and nurses were pouring over me, prodding and poking, speaking a totally foreign tongue, and there was no vision to compensate. Thoughts of 'What if I am blind' abounded, as well as wondering 'How I was going to get home' as my charter flight would not wait for me. I realised the next day that insurance covers the latter with a flight home courtesy of Mars Ltd., who as a World Cup sponsor, had numerous shuttles of guests going to and from Italy. My eyes recovered over the next few days, thanks to some yellow dyed medicine injected into them, but if anyone ever wants to be genuinely scared I would suggest being blindfolded for an hour in surroundings they do not know, never mind abroad, and see how it feels. This experience made me realise just how extraordinary blind people must be in even attempting to lead a normal life, but once recovered the only thing on my mind was, 'where next?'

England had drawn Turkey, Republic of Ireland, and Poland in a qualifying group; with the winners securing a finals trip to Sweden in 1992. I attended every qualifying match and with the Poland game, which was staged in Poznan in November 1991, saw the talismanic Gary Lineker score an equalising goal, thirteen minutes from time, which sent England to Sweden. I also saw other, more disturbing issues.

Elements of England support were looking to fight, and hurling parts of the decrepit seating onto the pitch; whilst aiming at the police and army. I had noticed the fighting in Ireland the previous autumn, when there were over a hundred arrests, but felt it was cut both ways, particularly given the political situation and the acknowledged 'far-right' political elements active within football supporters.

Second, I noticed the appalling poverty of the majority of the Poznan public. The lights did not burn brightly (the reasons I will detail later), and the hotel was basic to say the least, but my overriding non-football memory concerned a young female.

The coach from the airport; no, the landing strip with a hut in the corner, was stuck at some traffic lights by a square. There were numerous vendors positioned in pre-fabricated stands by the lights.

I later found out via a German girlfriend, Daniela Kloss who grew up in communist East Germany, that owning one of these stands, particularly in the old Soviet republics (and satellite states as well) was a sign of a person's wealth and capitalist ideals, but back in Poznan, one stall was selling bananas. A young student type bought one and ate it as if it was best Beluga caviar. This brought home the lack of luxuries eminent in post-communist Poland and how lucky the student was in the fact she could afford a banana and how lucky I was in that a plane was waiting to take me home two days later. Daniella explained that the food consumed in the former communist bloc was either 'grey', including the meat and carrots, or from a tin can, and that the nearest the citizens of East Germany ever came to 'coloured' food was tinned tangerines.

During this trip, I met some 'mates', with whom I would travel abroad over the next couple years. Lee Scott was from Flitwick, and told of us of the time he spent a week locked up at the pleasure of the Hungarian authorities eating onion stew with mouldy bread and running impromptu English classes for his fellow inmates. His travel partner Doug, also a Liverpool fan, shall I say, was more 'spaced' out and not an England 'regular'.

I was travelling alone and the travel company 'twinned' roommates for the hotel. I was with Troy Trubritt who was a QPR supporter and I have to say, was a real 'dead on' guy, for he was happy to help me pay a hotel bill when we went to watch England play in the USA, after the tour operator had not booked me into any of the hotels. The operator, based in Essex, appeared to carry out numerous tricks like this and was the subject of a BBC Watchdog investigation following the 1994 World Cup finals. It helped me to make a decision regarding future away travel, in that I would book all my own flights and hotels through a travel agent, and latterly via the Internet.

Watching the England team of the early 1990s was fun because I had met some good travelling companions, and was enjoying the novelty (then) of travelling, but two things were worrying. The team was struggling with Graham Taylor at the helm, playing bizarre formations with the likes of Manchester United winger Lee Sharpe at wing back, and the nemesis of this was a 2-0 loss to the USA in Boston in June 1993. Secondly, the violence prior to England games in Oslo and Rotterdam and during the match in Izmir, when a travelling companion lost an eye, caused by a missile thrown from a Turkish fan, was slowly causing me to make decisions on whether it was safe watching England play. Some supporters seemed at their happiest intimidating the local police or fighting amongst themselves with, from the little I saw, Chelsea and Leeds supporters often being at the centre of affairs.

My decision to 'give up' came inside a dumpster behind a bar in Amsterdam in the afternoon prior to the England v Holland game in Rotterdam. Troy, Lee, Doug and others were having a quiet drink in a bar when all hell broke loose outside and it immediately became every man for himself. Troy and I ran through the kitchen and hid in the industrial rubbish bin outside until the commotion died down. Watershed time had arrived, compounded by the fact England, perhaps unluckily, lost 2-0. I went to watch England play San Marino in Bologna, the game made famous by the home side scoring after nine seconds, only because I had paid to, and by now the events of February 1993 were playing on my mind.

I did watch England play one further game abroad: though it later deemed not to be a real game because it was in Dublin in February 1995 and abandoned after 30 minutes with one wrecked stadium and fingers pointing at England's so called 'supporters'. With hindsight, one has to ask who decided to play this highly volatile fixture inside a rugby ground with no proper crowd segregation. Enough said!

On 17th February 1993, England was playing San Marino at Wembley, but also Northern Ireland was playing Albania in Tirana. The events and characters on this trip made it much easier, if ease is the correct word, to 'convert' my international support.

A FIRST TIME FOR EVERYTHING

The planning for my first foray with Northern Ireland began in a dingy office at Whitelands College in London in October 1992, where I was the college bar manager, busily creating a viable business proposition after years of mismanagement and neglect. It was a position I fell into, as the premises needed a manager and I needed some money in recession savaged post-Thatcher Britain, where jobs were few, even for those with a so-called 'degree'.

When I first rang the IFA to enquire if any supporters clubs were planning a trip to Albania, I was advised to ring their travel agent, West End Travel, whose offices were in also in London. Manager David Segal seemed happy to allow me to travel as there was to be a small group of supporters allowed on the charter, along with players, press and officials, on one condition. I had to get a reference from both the England Travel Club/FA, of which I was a member, and my employers. Jill Smith, who managed the Travel Club, and my line manager both duly obliged and the rendezvous was confirmed for Luton Airport on the morning of 17th February.

1993, was pre budget-airlines, and as such Luton Airport appeared a cold, featureless and empty hanger, quite literally on top of a hill. A Monarch Airlines check-in desk was besieged with males in tracksuits, above which was a television monitor, informing all of destination Tirana. I felt in awe of checking in with personalities seen on television: the likes of Jack Charlton, The Republic of Ireland manager on a scouting mission, Northern Ireland manager Billy Bingham and players like Queens Park Ranger's captain Alan McDonald.

The plane seating plan placed me next to respected Daily Telegraph journalist Christopher Davies, who summed up the vibes of the trip to Albania in his copy the proceeding Friday by saying, "You knew it was going to be one of those trips...when the pilot had to re-adjust his landing because a farmer was tending his sheep across the runway."

My mother, when asking where I was going in the world, always used to say 'Be careful!', but she gave up after I recounted some of the visions I saw in my 27 hours in Tirana. I saw a cold, hungry looking and hopeless people, who had dug roots out of the ground, from long gone trees, to burn for warmth: children begging for sweets (or anything else) at the airport and fighting over oranges given to them by other supporters. The main hotel suffered on-going power cuts, leaving IFA officials stuck in the lift, and the press / supporters hotel had no windows, lights, or running water - save for leaky taps! I, and other supporters had to seek solace on the floors of those 'lucky' enough to stay in the Hotel Tirana.

However, three memories will be with me forever; one of which is the main cause of this book.

On the Tuesday evening, when the party arrived at the hotel, there was a request by IFA General Secretary, David Bowen, for any of the supporters with catering experience to report to on-board chef Tom Nesbitt, who needed help in the kitchen, as the Albanian authorities had decided not to offer help in the form of catering staff. The other supporters were requested to carry foodstuffs to the kitchen or 'safe' rooms, as it was likely to go 'missing'. Having worked in kitchens during college vacations, I offered my services, as requested, and ended up cooking bread in a stone oven, and attempting to boil potatoes on a gas hob with heat the strength of a match. Steak and roast chicken, two veg, and, yes, boiled potatoes and hot bread did eventually appear 110 times.

Quite how, I am still not sure, but it was humbling to see the Albanian staff sorting through the leftovers and putting peas and carrots back into the respective pots for future use.

The second memory occurred in the cold light of match day morning following a night of sickness due to my own stupidity; down to drinking Albanian tap water when thirsty. The phrase 'Sorry, Sir I didn't think', when you did something wrong at school springs to mind.

I wanted to mail some postcards home, for no other reason than to say I had visited this place. A small shop in the hotel lobby furnished the cards, but alas there were no stamps. On exiting the hotel, searching for a post office, a young boy called Gerti accosted me, offering any help I required. I said I needed stamps and he seemingly frog-marched me across town to the post office, and to the front of a queue on arrival. A similar march back to the hotel soon followed and then the horse-trading began. By helping me, Gerti wanted dollars and lots of them. I gave him ten, and he replied by suggesting he needed more. I held my guns, thinking he had just earned a month's salary for twenty minutes work, but took his address, saying I would send him something from Britain noting his dreadfully torn trainers.

The cards arrived some five weeks later, but I have often felt guilty that I never sent him at least a new pair of shoes, seeking some kind of rescue from this guilt by thinking that some guy in the Albanian post office would steal any package with British stamps on. Also, Gerti was streetwise and his skills in English would probably have seen him through those desperate times.

Thirdly, and most importantly, a broken bottle of water caused by Tirana airport baggage handlers literally throwing our baggage off the plane, meant I happened upon two supporters; names of Gavin Nixon and Clarke Gibson.

A typical Eastern European airport 'passport' delay led me to be in a queue behind the said persons. Gavin noticed my bag leaking courtesy of the above and once the shattered bottle of Ballygowan was removed the pleasantries began. The 'why watch Northern Ireland?' question came out and then Gavin suggested that I should come to Northern Ireland to watch a football match. He repeated a similar question in a similar queue on departure and I said something like 'Sure'. Whatever Northern Ireland was, or was going to be like, bearing in mind the IRA were still organising what they termed 'spectaculars', where high profile attacks blew Protestant market towns to smithereens, nothing could be as bad as this place. I decided on the flight home that I would not bullshit Gavin in coming to Northern Ireland, and would not leave my food again, showing some sort of solidarity with starving Albanians, whilst also having some inner satisfaction that I had slain the monkey of visiting Albania.

For the record, Northern Ireland beat Albania 2-1; thanks to a penalty kick late in the second half. I like to think I took a photo of that incident, but soon after returning home, the communal house I shared with two others in Wimbledon Park was burgled and the camera, inclusive of a half reel of Albanian film, plus the all-important collector's bank note, was stolen. I did get some pictures of the Albania experience via Gavin. They were black and white; as the X-ray machine was so dated it discoloured any camera film. That summed Albania up; colourless and featureless, but my mind was made up. I would see the last rites of England's qualifying campaign, for no other reason that I had paid deposits on the trips, and then take my holidays to both home (Belfast) and away trips. The insistence, the taunting of Gavin Nixon, and the camaraderie endured on this trip was infectious.

BOSTON FOR A WEEKEND

The European football calendar operates in two yearly cycles, summer football festivals, entailing the World Cup and European (Nations) Cup take place around the globe in even ending years. For those nations not fortunate enough to be at the party, the crumbs incorporate a round of 'fodder' friendlies against those who qualified, providing little more than match practice. For the Germans, a perennial qualifier, it may mean a morale, goal-scoring boost against the likes of part-time neighbours Liechtenstein. In May 1994, it meant Northern Ireland taking a trip to Boston to play a dark horse for the World Cup, in Colombia.

At the time, I was beginning to do some non-football soul-searching in that I was becoming increasingly bored and frustrated with work and decided I needed a break. Cue a trip on the fledgling airline, Virgin Atlantic, free ice creams and all, to watch the game.

I had travelled to the US in the previous summer, but had little chance to acclimatise to Boston as we moved on to Washington within 48 hours.

In my opinion, the US (and Boston) equals big: cars, highways, skyscrapers, burgers, shops, and, in particular, people.

I managed to get a ticket to watch the Boston Red Sox whilst in town, and sat beside a pleasant family who quite simply watched and ate for the four-hour duration. Chips, (Fenway) frankfurters, bagels, candyfloss, soft drinks and beer; all, it appeared as merely nibbles. I would leave their (big) waist size to one's imagination, but sat in amazement as Texas Ranger hitter Jose Conseco launched a 'home-run', which was still going up as it sailed over the 'Big Green Monster' some 325 feet away.

Northern Ireland were revealing a new dawn, as Bryan Hamilton had recently been appointed the new manager and begun his reign with wins over Romania and Liechtenstein. Colombia was a different deal, full of household stars, including (Scorpion) goalkeeper Rene Huiguita, fuzzy haired playmaker Carlos Valderamma, and the Newcastle bound striker Faustino Asprilla. A young Northern Ireland team, which included a winger named Keith Gillespie, who many thought could, just maybe, become the next George Best, were respectable in only losing 2-0.

On the Monday flight home, I decided I needed a new job; though this was somewhat peripheral in my thinking, as I was still on a football high and looking forward to my next Northern Ireland experience: a first trip to Belfast to watch a Euro'96 qualifier against Portugal.

THE FIRST TIME

Gavin Nixon had been true to his word and had bought me a 'season ticket' for the Euro'96 qualifying series. This had begun with a 4-1 victory over Liechtenstein in April, but the 'real' business (and the season ticket) began with a fixture against Portugal in September.

I was living (briefly) at Mum's in Lytham at the time and flew from Blackpool to Belfast, for what, as explained, was a jump into the unknown.

Northern Ireland is different from the mainland in that it has its own banknotes, its own bread, as soda and potato bread are to die for, its own breakfast, the wonderfully cholesterol filled 'Ulster fry', great fish and chips (from Gavin's favourite 'Friar Tuck' just off the Newtonards Road) and fantastic character filled pubs. For a jump into the unknown, it was a great one and, as mentioned, not the fear-filled bullet dodging place I was led to believe. Even the bus drivers said 'Hello': such a difference from the anonymity of London and Wimbledon, where I lived for four years and never even knew the name, let alone spoke to, the next door neighbour. I quickly realised this was due to the community spirit that exists throughout Northern Ireland. In Ulster's small villages and towns, it appears there is still a butcher, baker, florist and the like, rather than the anonymous mass consumerism of supermarkets and shopping malls that has destroyed trades and communities on the mainland.

Like most football 'crowds', Gavin and his friends met up and journeyed to Windsor Park together. The meeting house was The Crown Liquor saloon in Great Victoria

Street. The hostelry stands near the Belfast Europa Hotel, which has the dubious record of being the most 'bombed' hotel in the world. When I saw the hotel, memories of pre-pubescent evenings in front of the television news came back, especially as the hotel was in the throes of being re-built. It was kind of a memorial landmark as far as I was concerned.

As for The Crown, it was a gas lamp lit Victorian bar with drinking booths and brass rails, along with an incredibly ornate marble floor. I latterly found out, it is owned by the National Trust and has numerous preservation orders on its various fixtures. I took David Charlut there on a visit in 2000, and he was quite literally gob-smacked. The Guinness is also pretty good too. Marketed in 1994 as 'the big pint' in Northern Ireland, the Guinness was (and is) poured in a glass to ¾ full, left for around four minutes, money taken, and then topped up, with a typical head that holds itself above the glass. I will leave the adjectives of taste to others; save to say the Crown's Guinness and that served in other Ulster hostelries is unique and amazing. It is also 'cheap' in relative terms, for on the mainland stout is a 'premium' product, hence the price is comparable to that of Stella and Kronenbourg. In Northern Ireland it appears to be part of staple diet, with a price to match.

Gavin's friends, most of who were his work-mates, duly arrived and the pre-match festivities began, concluding with a mile and a half hike to Windsor Park, via a car park in Sandy Row and the Lisburn Road. Over the years, this evolved in to occasional stop-offs at a chip shop in Sandy Row, various off-licences, and the now non-existent Four in Hand pub on the Lisburn Road, which has become a (trendy) wine bar called Ryan's.

Gavin decided that I was to be called John, because the implications of being called a Shaun (which I later researched was a Scottish version and IS the equivalent of the Gaelic spelt Sean) in Windsor Park could be serious.

Put simply, the political situation in Northern Ireland meant (and still does) that the Roman Catholic population in Northern Ireland are largely ambivalent to the fortunes of the national football team and generally lean their loyalties to the Republic of Ireland team. Therefore someone being called Shaun, watching Northern Ireland at Windsor Park, in a solidly Protestant audience may cause an issue. It never has done, as I have explained my situation to a great many people when necessary; who often retort with 'You are very welcome', or 'We need more supporters like you!'. Nevertheless, Gavin's reasoning was fair meaning and John was fortunately rarely used, with Shaun with an 'H' quickly becoming a christened phrase.

I felt Gavin's concern was vindicated when I took my place in the South Stand at Windsor Park. The ground could be considered 'dated' at best, with one (goal) end closed, due to UEFA regulations forbidding standing terraces, and another housing both terracing and a dilapidated 300 seat stand, which is named the 'Railway Stand'. Sited on the stadium fencing was a banner suggesting, 'NO CEASEFIRE AT WINDSOR PARK!'

The week prior to my initial visit was tumultuous in the history of Northern Ireland in that the Provisional IRA had declared a unilateral 'cessation of activities'. Optimism abounded, with politicians suggesting self-rule (as Northern Ireland had been governed directly from Westminster since 1972) and moderate Catholic and Protestant leaders shook hands with the gusto of long lost brothers. Therefore such a banner was worrying, as were the chanting of so-called 'party songs', such as the 'Sash', and the 'Billy-Boys' which are anthems for the more hard-line Ulster loyalists. I was more used to hearing England supporters suggesting 'the Falklands were ours' (when playing Argentina) and that any mainland European nation would be 'Krauts' (Germans) if not for the English, although renditions of supporters not surrendering to the IRA did occasionally appear.

However, the present day optimism did win the day and those banners and tunes are thankfully replaced with requests to rid football of sectarianism and vocal support for the team, which usually contains Catholic players.

As for the game, Northern Ireland lost 2-1, giving away a very 'soft' goal late on. The history of this group, the prize being qualification for the European finals in England in summer 1996, eventually showed this cost Northern Ireland dear because they finished tied for second with the Republic of Ireland. Simply, an extra point would have sent the team into a play off for a place in England against a crack Holland side. All ifs and buts I know, but it does not stop me dreaming.

Walking back to Hunter's Bar, which is the nearest bar to Windsor Park, I was surprised at the physical state of the ground. A new Spion stand has latterly appeared (in 1997), but it is somewhat embarrassing to visit so-called 'poor' countries in Armenia, Romania and even mid 90s Lithuania, who have better facilities. Of course, politics rears its head here, particularly in Eastern Europe where governments are often proud of fledgling nationhood and see fit to invest in national stadiums, to create a modicum of flag-waving at national events. Fiascos over the cost of a new Wembley Stadium, a Millennium Dome, or the fact Britain could not host a World Athletics Championships in 2005 because of stadium funding problems, bear out the point that British governments are not prepared to invest in their nation. Hence the state of Windsor Park, which has depended on lottery funding for any improvements.

The rest of this trip was dominated by a tour of Northern Ireland via Gavin's ageing Vauxhall Nova. The imposing Belfast City Hall, which I formally visited in 2002, and the equally impressive Stormont Parliament building were tempered by the inner city poverty of the Nationalist Divis and Loyalist Shankill, complete with terrace-end murals. I was amazed at the intricacy of these murals, which suggested Para-military groups were the local defenders of tradition. The reasoning, sociology and work involved behind murals and bunting belongs elsewhere, save to say artwork in inner city Northern Ireland did, and does appear to be a growth industry.

Other car-stops incorporated the affluence and beauty of Holywood, Helen's Bay, the Antrim Coast and the Portrush beaches and the not so pretty Bogside corner of Londonderry, complete with tricolour flying from a pole above a permanent edifice stating 'You are now entering free Derry': with this comment suggesting Northern Ireland is occupied by British agents. Looking across at this area from the walls of Derry, I could understand why, after a visit to Northern Ireland, Home Secretary Reginald Maudling once said, 'What a bloody awful place. Pour me a large scotch!' Having lived in various inner-cities notably Wolverhampton and a racially divisive Luton, I can concur with this view. Despite this, I have always found the people of Northern Ireland genuinely warm and friendly from whichever side of the religious divide, even at the mentioned Bogside Corner, where two young mothers both said 'Hello', as they walked their youngsters home. Nowadays, I send more Christmas cards to Ulster than to mainland Britain.

TRIPS, BUTS AND MAYBES

Group draws, to create the qualifying series for European and World Cup Finals are often pedantic affairs, but the usual scenario incorporates over-hyped football and future host nation luminaries plucking balls out of separated oversized brandy glasses. The glasses contain eight or nine balls with the names of countries inside and broadly the standard of countries' results over the previous few years qualifying series determines which 'seeding' glass a nation is in. Hence, the likes of France Germany and Italy, perennial qualifiers, are top seeds and Luxembourg, Malta and San Marino are in the 'dead weight' pot. The ultimate idea therefore is that the best nations always qualify at the expense of the weak.

However, qualification for Euro'96 was more unique, in that the top two nations in each group qualified, save the two nations placed second with the weakest record, which played off for a place: this game being the Ireland v Holland game. The hosts (England) were the sixteenth team to make up the party. This expansion allows the chance for some of the lesser lights to get a place at the top table and boost their respective seeding. Romania, Bulgaria, Latvia, Slovenia and Norway have benefited from this scenario.

In 1993, Northern Ireland had not qualified for a final series for seven years (since 1986) and was considered a respective third or fourth seed pot team. This ultimately meant Northern Ireland had Portugal, Republic of Ireland, and Austria seeded above them and Latvia and Liechtenstein below them in the Euro'96 group.

Occasions of qualifying draws, allow the likes of me, who are perhaps a football rarity in I that I do not have a club to support, an opportunity to dream. This is because I can fantasise about where I am going on holiday over the next eighteen months. Do you fly far away to the peripheries of Europe and endure the culture and poverty of the Armenia and Moldova's or do you wish for 'home-derbies' against England or the Republic? I am reasonably non-committal, save I am always very much in favour of visits to rarefied Iceland and ambivalent to hot-countries such as Spain and in particular Turkey, where a travelling partner lost an eye during a riot inside the ground in Izmir in 1991. I am also eagerly awaiting Russia to come out of a glass and be paired with Northern Ireland.

Bearing this in mind, the countries in the group provided a reasonable cross section and the next stop off was an away trip to Austria.

I travelled with three England supporters of old to Vienna, as there was an opportunity to watch a competitive England team play, as well as Northern Ireland. This was because Northern Ireland then had no under-21 team, whilst England, as Euro'96 hosts, had no group qualification and the Under-21 team, who had to qualify for their respective finals, needed a slot. They therefore took Northern Ireland's place in a mirrored Under-21 group.

Doug, Lee, Troy and I set off on 3 day Monday to Thursday city break to Vienna. In 1994, there were no budget airways, which now run simple and cheap bus services in the air. Air travel was very much a trait of business, with discounted fares only available if a Saturday night was included, or a 3 day inclusive hotel trip package was booked through an accommodating travel agent.

If the thoughts included in this book are ever to be used as some kind of tourist guide, then one piece of advice I am happy to give is to stay away from Vienna's nightlife on Monday nights. Four guys arrive and go out on the town looking for a bit of fun, with a few drinks, some banter with the locals, and some music and 'window shopping'. In this context, 'window-shopping' means eyeing up the local female talent and making a move if you have enough courage, mostly boosted by alcohol, to make a simple pass. In all of these contexts however, Vienna was shut.

The nearest we got to a pub (or bar/tavern) with atmosphere was a place that was like a glorified living room; curtains and all. There were a lot of people in the place and we thought it was the happening place and began chatting loudly to 'up' the atmosphere. A bar maid came over and told us to be quiet and we questioned her request. Then a burly male came across, who spoke English, and said if we wanted to stay in the premises, we MUST be quiet. The reason shortly became clear as a pre-pubescent girl entered the room, complete with violin, and began a recital, hastening our departure to the hotel bar around six hours before anticipated.

The day after was dominated by the trip to Kaftenburg, for the Austria v England U-21 game. After this, Lee and co., decided to try to fly home as they did not want to suffer any more of the Viennese boredom.

I naturally stayed to watch the Northern Ireland game in the Happel Stadion, Austria's national stadium.

Northern Ireland won 2-1; in a game, which was memorable for a Keith Gillespie strike after only four minutes, which was not dissimilar to the one regularly repeated and scored by Marco van Baasten in the 1988 European Championship final. However, the real hero was goalkeeper Paul Kee, who was then keeping for Irish League part-timers Ards. Kee had kept for clubs in the lower strata's of the English league, such as Hull, and his performance that night was one typical of a giant-killing act in the F.A. Cup, where legs, arms, head and all somehow seem to get in the way of the ball, preventing the favourites taking the spoils.

On my next return to Northern Ireland, I also noticed a 'political' storm, of which Ulster is famed had come and gone over the television coverage from Austria. Host broadcaster ORF, had shown captions of Northern Ireland players with the Republic of Ireland's flag by them. Being English I was, and am, used to the Union Jack being misinterpreted as England's flag, but in Northern Ireland this is a serious act of misjudgement. In short, flag waving is important in Northern Ireland amongst both traditions, as can be seen from flag-poles, street lamps and the like and cannot seemingly be compromised.

Talking of the Republic, the next game was a Windsor Park fixture against them in November.

Northern Ireland lost this game 4-0, which was a major embarrassment to all concerned and quickly became a forgettable occasion, save an incident on the way to the ground.

Copious amounts of Guinness had been drunk during the day and on the way up the Lisburn Road, I felt there was no alternative but to relieve myself against a back alley wall. After re-adjusting myself, I turned to face an army officer pointing a rifle at my midriff. A pee-break almost became a full-blown impromptu ablution as the officer demanded to know my business. A hurried explanation and severe rollicking followed, but it made me realise the vigilance the security forces had to keep, for despite the so-called ceasefire, the place I had decided to pee was probably not dissimilar to where a Para-military punishment would take place.

To those with inkling for political cynicism, it should always be noted that there has never really been a ceasefire in Northern Ireland. Sure, there has been a major cessation since 1994, with market towns and villages (except for Omagh in 1998) not, quite literally, having their guts blown out, but there are still many 'punishments', often incorporating a bullet through a knee or a baseball bat attack, carried out by those with deviant interests.

DUBLIN AND DERBIES

The police in Dublin, which was Northern Ireland's next stop off in March 1995, certainly do not carry guns and the army is non-existent as regards supporting daily law and order.

Prior to this, England attempted to play an international in Lansdowne Road in mid February.

This ground was, and probably still is, not fit to host what would be a highly charged, albeit friendly, international. It is known as the oldest international rugby stadium in the world, (is often windswept and muddy) and suited to the oval balls' camaraderie, rather than football's intensity and rivalry. There has been little crowd segregation and on my three visits, crowd control has relied and hoped on bodies being in the way rather than fencing.

England had played competitive matches against the Republic of Ireland in the European Finals in 1988 (1-0 to Republic) in Italy in World Cup'90 (1-1 draw) and twice in the qualifying series for the 1992 European Finals (both 1-1 draws) and as such the favourites to win had been undone by the 'Celtic' underdog. This series of results was perhaps not so surprising, as the Republic, under the tutelage of 1966 World Cup winner Jack Charlton, had used FIFA rules on national qualification to build a competitive team built around regular England and Scotland top league players. Not surprisingly the Irish contingent would goad the England supporters, some of whom had quite openly racist opinions and thuggish intentions, with chants such as 'You'll never beat the Irish', countered by the English contingent suggesting there should be 'No surrender to the IRA'. Football wise, the end result was a cocktail of crowd intimidation and simmering hostility, which boiled over when the Republic scored after 25 minutes. The ground and authorities could not cope: a stand got wrecked, the ground was invaded and the match was abandoned. In hindsight, as hinted, it was nonsense to play such a game, with the aforementioned ingredients, but personally this meant Lansdowne Road was not really a place in early spring for an Englishman supporting Northern Ireland.

However, I had decided to go this game a long time before the February hiatus. The IFA had decided not to sell tickets for the game. I believe a reciprocal arrangement had been in operation the previous November with the 'away' association not being allocated tickets. This led to Winston Rea, one of the main luminaries in the Shankill Supporters Club picketing the IFA's Windsor Avenue offices in protest. A small group of supporters, inclusive of the Shankill did get an 'invitation' to the game via a Republic's supporters' group, but as for myself I had no option but to tout a ticket.

Those in the 'know', especially rugby supporters, had told me to get up early and surf O'Connell Street, which is like Dublin's equivalent of Regent Street, and the touts will be conspicuous. Soon after 7.30 a.m. a £IR65 exchange for an £IR18 ticket occurred and I was in. Then the worries started.

Last time the stadium was used for a soccer match, the ground was wrecked courtesy of an English mob and here was a solitary Englishman watching Northern Ireland in what was a lonely foreign den. Save to say, I said little throughout and did not cheer when Ian Dowie met a Keith Gillespie cross mid way through the second half to level the game at 1-1. I wasn't frightened as I was seated in a family type enclosure in the South Stand, just felt it better to keep my own counsel and look forward to openly supporting the team in Latvia a month hence.

I THINK IT WAS IN THE SOVIET UNION

In 2004, budget airline Ryanair started running bus-flights to Latvian capital Riga, as this once disaffected Soviet satellite republic became assimilated in to a new empire, namely the European Union (and all that goes with it!). However, in 1995, travel to this country, somewhere past Finland, but not quite in Russia was somewhat more difficult.

I had found an East European travel specialist in East Anglia, who was not involved with Inntourist, the former Soviet government run travel operation who charged the earth to see the Soviet sites, such as the Kremlin and St..Petersburg. Gunnel Travel was a family operation run by Terence and Gunnel Billing who were very sincere and helpful in getting me to Riga and explained at some length the vagaries of going to the former Soviet Union, whilst latterly laughing at my expense by mailing post-it labels when I booked future trips. This was because, whilst packing and loading the car from Stourbridge in the West Midlands to Heathrow, I left my plane tickets and hotel voucher on the roof of the car and drove off with them blowing in the wind: or so to speak.

A good tip in gauging a country's wealth is by seeing how brightly the lights burned. A rule of thumb is that the further East in Europe you dig, the darker the lights, as there is less electric generated. The visits to Poland and the Czech Republic had shown how a nation was attempting to throw off the shackles of universal poverty inflicted by communism and their bulbs along with Riga's, but only to a point, did not burn very brightly. I say to a point, because I was further informed that the new Baltic States, particularly Estonia and Latvia received aid, pre and post Cold war from near neighbours Finland.

The negatives of the country were the poor begging, like Albania in 1993, and a general standard of living which saw raw, fly ridden meat being sold in Riga's street market. The positives were the sight of hordes of beautiful mini-skirted women going around their business, a McDonald's (well any port in a storm as Robert Walsh in Donetsk in 2003 will further testify), a young pre-pubescent interpreter cum entrepreneur called Gerti (yes another one-with the same name as the Albanian youngster) and bumping into Marty Lowry.

I will always remember this guy Gerti who announced himself as being fluent in seven languages, inclusive of English and American, as well as being able to supply girls, guns, drugs and black market champagne. I just wanted more goals in the Latvians net than ours, but it wouldn't surprise me now if Gerti were an e-industry millionaire milking the European Union dry. Not even Marty could supply that, but he informed me, as we got to know each other, that he ultimately wanted to produce an off the wall fanzine magazine dedicated to the Northern Ireland team. In various guises, Our Wee Country has been produced in both paper form and latterly on the Internet; with Marty appearing on radio, in magazines and working ceaselessly to raise the profile of Northern Ireland's football team around the world. Also, his internet work has helped give many people the chance to watch Northern Ireland, by arranging trips and tours for less regular supporters. Though perhaps not my personal cup of tea, as the Our Wee Country trips usually incorporate copious amounts of drinking, Marty should always be known as a grade one guy, complete with an ever-present file.

Marty, myself, Gerti and numerous members of the Shankill club, left the Daugavas Stadium, complete with shale running track and imposing 'Soviet' style floodlights, having seen Northern Ireland grind out a 1-0 victory, thanks to an Ian Dowie penalty.

CANADA AND BEXHILL!

Work wise; Granada Entertainments had employed me, since autumn 1994 in a management capacity. By spring 1995, an internal opportunity arose in Bexhill and the move from Brierley Hill, a downtrodden suburb of Dudley in the West Midlands, occurred at the same time as a three cornered competition in Edmonton, Canada, which involved Northern Ireland. As a young, and then ambitious manager, I wanted to impress and decided to miss the trip to Canada. With hindsight, I wish I had not bothered, as I quickly began to realise that often big businesses may talk a good game, but are merely brutal money making machines and care little about whom they employ and their social surroundings. I am not ashamed to say the owner's senior management saw fit to bully and harass me, whilst at Bexhill, and could not understand that the punters who lived around, and visited the quaint but dated geriatric filled town wanted to enjoy the hottest summer for twenty years and not go ten-pin bowling in a non-air conditioned hanger. In short, the bowling alley did not take enough money and that did not suit those in suits.

As such, I decided that in the future work would not get in the way of my burgeoning hobby of travel / football and to date it never has done as I have been careful to choose employers who are small, often family orientated, with a cohesive group of staff. Company directors will think nothing of going on corporate golf days, so I do not see a problem in my doing it: officially of course. I openly accept it has cost me financially, but whilst important, money is not my main motivation. Without getting into psychological profiling I consider life too short to spend every waking hour chained to a desk trying to a get better hire-purchase car in the drive.

My new found attitude rancoured once too often in 1996, when a pre-booked 10 day holiday to take in most of Euro 96, was destroyed by an over zealous regional manager who saw fit to ignore my written (and accepted) holiday request, as he needed to redevelop his corporate affairs. Pity that, as I took a month off sick on full pay with stress and also had great delight in creating an annoyance scale, whereby the company was punished. If I was shouted at, I threw a box of burgers in the bin on my way home, upping that to a box of scampi if the 'offence' included swearing. Eventually, a 3-month redundancy package was agreed with my so-called 'entertainment centre' overlords and we went our separate ways.

I was, of course, deflated over missing the Canada trip, but Northern Ireland did have a return fixture in Belfast in early June against Latvia, and I decided that Northern Ireland were now to come first in sports spectating terms, even at the expense of salad days spent at Lords cricket ground.

That Wednesday night in June, was dreadful as Northern Ireland lost 1-2, to then, as mentioned, a poor, part-time team. So acute the embarrassment that Arthur Chetter, one of Gavin's work-mates walked away from Windsor Park, never to be seen again. With hindsight, I saw the game as a football watershed.

(International) football pundits, particularly on television, always drone on when 'big' teams struggle, saying 'there are no easy games', and 'you cannot take the new European teams lightly', but in this case, it was a correct comment. Latvia, a nation only admitted to the UEFA table in 1992, could rightly then be considered a group make-weight, in that they were expected to beat total amateurs Liechtenstein, but cause few problems to the professional teams, especially away from home. The fact they beat Northern Ireland, meant they and other 'new' teams such as Estonia and Slovenia, were organizing nationally and on the 'up' in football terms; culminating with qualification for Euro 2004, in the case of Latvia and Euro 2000 and the 2002 World Cup for Slovenia. As for Northern Ireland, the spiral was in the opposite direction, as they slowly became a nation who most other teams would be expected to take points off; inclusive of the likes of Liechtenstein.

When playing golf with my Dad, the phrase 'If I hadn't done that then this....', would often be used and retorted by him suggesting 'That if my aunt had been my uncle, then she would have had balls!', or 'It's called golf not IF!' I thought about the former phrase as the group developed, because as mentioned, 'If this group had panned out the same way but Northern Ireland had beaten or even drawn against Latvia, they would have at least had a play-off game to part-take in to qualify for the party in England the following summer. Since then, Northern Ireland has never looked like qualifying for a final series and the huge financial rewards that go with a journey to a final series.

For the record, this is also the start of this ten year journey in watching Northern Ireland's every game: the next stop being a trip to Porto in late summer for the Portugal fixture.

It was here that I began to feel less of an outsider looking in on Northern Ireland.

I have mainly travelled abroad on my own save for Robert Walsh and other 'occasionals', with whom I know, because I consider these trips my Ceauceascu holidays, an escape from the 9 to 5 merry-go-round, and as such will get up when I want to get up and do what I want to do. This may not suit others and therefore it is best to go it alone. However, I was beginning to bump into the same supporters abroad, and sharing meals, and more especially drinks with groups such as the 1st Shankill Northern Ireland Supporters Club. Indeed after a night out with Shankill luminaries Winston Rea, 'Flint', Phillip King et al in Porto, I can vaguely remember falling asleep standing upright whilst waiting for my key at 7.00 a.m. in the hotel after a blatantly heavy night.

I began to notice two major differences in England and Northern Ireland supporters. First was the age, in that most supporters seemed middle-aged rather than young 'laddish' types you might meet on a Friday night in any town centre. Second the supporters stick together and appear to have little inter-club rivalry, save a little harmless banter, whereas England supporters often travel in 'club' groups and have, from first sight, got drunk in foreign cities and gone looking for supporters to settle an old club score. Whether it still occurs, is to find elsewhere, but in the early 90s groups of West Ham, Millwall, Leeds and Chelsea supporters seemed never to be far away from trouble, often wearing club regalia. Bizarrely, though supporters I have seen abroad for the past ten years are never seen at home games. Robert Walsh sits in the Kop Stand at Windsor Park, and Justin and Paul Duffin, two travelling supporters from Doagh sit in the North Stand, whilst I have my position with Gavin Nixon's friends and work colleagues in front of the press box in the South Stand. With hindsight, I suppose the chances of seeing someone in a crowd of 11,000 is less than seeing that same person in a corner of an 'away' ground reserved for a few travelling supporters. Nevertheless this scenario does surprise me.

The game in Porto was played in the Stadio ground which greatly impressed me in that you entered the stadium and then went downwards from street level in to a huge atmospheric bowl, with groups of home supporters trading chants from the respective goal ends. Unfortunately for them, Northern Ireland ruined the party with an incredibly spirited 1-1 draw. It was expected that Northern Ireland would leak a few goals against the group favourites, who were being touted as a dark horse for the final party in England the following summer. From memory, the goal of Alan Fettis led a charmed life, a young Crewe midfielder called Neil Lennon featured significantly, and a thunderbolt free kick from Michael Hughes gave a spirited Northern Ireland a point. Obviously everyone was then asking 'Why didn't we do this against Latvia?', but we didn't and the rest, they say, is history.

LIECHTENSTEIN IS ROUND HERE SOMEWHERE!

Everybody who travels always takes great pleasure in describing their favourite place visited. Liz Pallace, my line manager at Remarkable Restaurants, suggests Venice, whilst my girlfriend loves the chicness of Paris. Until a second visit in 2002, I had always ranked Liechtenstein, along with the forests on the West coast of Jaellannd, Denmark, as my personal favourite. A return in 2002 had seen an almost obnoxious commercial highway built into capital Vaduz, complete with McDonald's and DIY hypermarkets, thereby knocking Liechtenstein off my own pedestal.

Back in 1995, I had booked with a Swiss tour operator to take me to this mountainous playground for the rich, which, sandwiched between Austria and Switzerland in the heart of The Alps, is often left off maps simply because it is so tiny: population 25,000, land mass 25 square miles.

To access the country, you fly to Zurich and take the train for 90 minutes to Buchs and then transfer by 'postbus': a bus literally carrying mail around the villages in the area, into the principality guarded by two flag poles holding the red and blue flags of the country. I arrived, found my hotel and then visited what was called, by locals, the 'city' (of Vaduz).

I had been told it was possible to get a stamp in a passport for Liechtenstein by visiting the post office in Vaduz, which was surrounded by tourist shops selling local trinkets, incorporating T-shirts, cow bells and local stamps, for which Liechtenstein is apparently renowned. True enough for 5 Swiss francs a stamp was franked onto page 6 of my passport and I asked the genteel 'stamper' where the offices of Liechtenstein F.A. were, as I decided it may have been an idea to get a match ticket. The lady said 'You will need to go and see Barbara!' and gave me directions to what was a very continental style, small block of apartments. I buzzed the bell and entered the front room of a lady's flat to find a football association laid out in little more than a front room. I bought my ticket and asked Barbara if she had any old match programmes, with me looking for a Republic of Ireland v Liechtenstein game, which was a 0-0 draw in early June (a result which caused much amusement amongst Northern Ireland supporters). She pointed me to a filing cabinet and now, not only being in a national associations head office, I was rifling through a filing cabinet, and eventually headed off with numerous match brochures, which were four-page fold out affairs.

The match day brochure was no different, with the game played in the Esschen Sportspark, which was merely a football ground in a field, with a post and rail fence, a 100 seat (at most) stand and changing rooms, and an edifice dedicated to the Pope's recent visit behind the goal at one end. Cows pastured behind the other goal in a field, whilst being watched over by the Royal Family's Schloss (or castle) which was on a mountain overlooking the entire Principality. Gavin Nixon latterly told me the BBC radio reporter described this whole scene, and forgot, save for a final prompt from the studio presenter to give the result: even describing the game played under an incredible blue sky in a atmosphere which was so clean it made your lungs burn if you fully inhaled. For the record, Northern Ireland won 4-0, finishing their travels in this group with an unbeaten record, which was probably the best of any nation in any group: playing five, winning three and drawing two. If only the home form was as formidable, although Northern Ireland did complete the series with a stunning 5-3 victory over Austria in Belfast.

Whilst the weather in Liechtenstein was stunningly beautiful, the weather in Belfast on that November night against Austria was disgusting. I can remember little about the game, apart from the tempest in which it was played and the fact I was wet through to my pants. I assumed Northern Ireland must have been magnificent to score five.

Gavin latterly showed me a video of the game, which justified its rank as the 38th best game ever in a Four Four Two magazine poll, but what was amusing was seeing BBC television commentators Jackie Fullerton, perhaps the Desmond Lynam of Ulster sports presenters, and (the) George Best trying to give a half-time analysis from a commentary box which resembled a Somme trench. Seeing that somehow made the torture I had to endure just to watch that match a little more bearable.

ATLAS ANYONE?

If I thought Liechtenstein was not on most people's atlas, then the draw for qualification for the World Cup finals in the summer of 1998, threw up an even more bizarre destination for Northern Ireland in Armenia. Now I consider myself educated, with a few qualifications and not shy when reading the foreign news in national newspapers, but even I had no idea where Armenia was. I knew it was a former Soviet republic, had an earthquake in 1988, and fought a war with its neighbour Azerbaijan around the same time. As for where it was, well any guesses! I did find out it was bordered by Turkey and Iran, and wondered how it could be considered in Europe, being the eastern outpost of UEFA's remit.

But the draw was done and Northern Ireland's other holiday destinations, from September 1996, would include Germany, Portugal, Ukraine and Albania. I think I just wrote holiday destinations. Albania!!!!

Beforehand, Northern Ireland had to provide the late spring friendly opposition for those qualified for Euro'96. Sweden and Norway visited Belfast before Germany in late May, which was poignant in that it was the last time the Spion Kop was to be stood on at an international. Years before, UEFA had prohibited standing at competitive internationals (you could sit on the grass in Liechtenstein!) and, as such countries with 'standing' national stadiums, like the Republic of Ireland's Lansdowne Road had to place temporary seating on terraces, but sanctioned standing was allowed at friendlies. Also, the Irish FA launched a new shirt at this match, which was a green and blue quartered top.

(United) Ireland, prior to the Republic's breakaway had played in navy blue, but recent times saw Northern Ireland playing in themes of green. Whether the incorporation of blue was a throwback or a contemporary design is open to question, but what was (and still is) popular amongst fans was the ensuing second, or away, strip. This was red and white quarters and, of course, closely resembled the national colours of the Ulster flag, to which the vast majority of Northern Ireland supporters are loyal. I have purchased every Northern Ireland strip since 1993, and though it rancours with my present girlfriend Rebecca, I insist on hanging up and regularly wearing each top, (to various functions including more formal receptions) and this one is by far my personal favourite. As an Englishman, it may be harder to answer as to specifically why, but the colours are incredibly deep and the design very unique.

Indeed I wore this top to the Euro'96 final between the Czech Republic and Germany, and it was at this event, that I began to feel absolute ambivalence towards the England football team. Do not get me wrong, I feel no ill will to those who support England or the team itself, but the issues and the hangers-on surrounding the team, especially at major tournament finals, is what I find most annoying. I find no need to read about team exploits in drinking clubs in Hong Kong or the clothes David Beckham has chosen for his team mates, or indeed the exploits of English people causing public order problems when England are defeated, usually on penalties, at a final series. Hence, I am not really bothered if England win, lose or otherwise at football. Often, and more regularly, as I have become known for following, Northern Ireland, people have asked whom I would support if England play Northern Ireland. My consistent answer is that I would get my ticket from the Irish F.A. and hope to sit in the Northern Ireland area, wearing a scarf in safety.

On the subject of getting tickets, Harry Simpson, with whom Gavin worked, had again arranged our group booking 'season' tickets for the Group 9 series, which began at the end of August 1996 and included the return of Saturday international fixtures after a gap of more than decade, as FIFA attempted to unify days and dates for the playing of international football.

The arranging of international qualifying series matches can be an arduous affair, with interested parties meeting in a designated city to thrash out fixtures on the mentioned pre-arranged dates. I have been told by Irish FA luminaries who attend these events that each country naturally has, and wants, their own agenda and arbitration can often be difficult particularly with East European countries. Indeed in the arguing the fixture dates for qualification for the Euro 2004 finals, Northern Ireland's group ceded to fixture draw by lots.

It appears Northern Ireland like to start with a home fixture, often against what may be perceived to be weak or 'poor' travelling countries, so as to get points on the board. As such, Ukraine and Armenia, both in Belfast were Northern Ireland's first opponents.

Results wise, things did not go to plan, as Northern Ireland lost 0-1 to Ukraine in August and only drew 1-1 against Armenia in early October. One point from six was not a successful return, particularly with Germany, the newly crowned European Champions coming up in Nuremberg in November.

I had booked to travel to Germany (Munich) from Luton airport with an airline that was to become one of the best friends of an international football supporter. Debonair, went broke shortly after I completed the trip, but their inception brought with it a host of other buses with wings offering cheap flights around Europe. Personally, it was a godsend, as I had recently taken a financial carrot from the 'entertainment' company, but a pay-off does not last forever, even if I did feel better health wise for doing it.

I had not realised how depressed all the swearing, harassment, and phone calls whilst on holiday had made me, and though money was now tight, I seemed a lot happier doing odd-jobs for Dad and Keith and Sarah Pollitt, who had just taken over a idyllic pub tenancy in North Wales; complete with goats and a donkey. The whole experience had taught me how contemptible bullying in the workplace is and not to get involved in it. I was unbelievably happy when, in 2000, shopping in Eastbourne, I found out the person who had carried out this personal crusade had been demoted to a negligible role for irregularities. Talk about what goes around coming around. I could name this guy, but do not want to stoop to his level, though in conclusion I will say I would want not to be him should we ever meet at a motorway service station.

However, in spectator terms, I was getting worried, when looking at forward planning for the far-off return trips to Ukraine and particularly Armenia. An aghast Thomas Cook representative in the Kidderminster branch had priced a midweek trip to Armenia, at £1,100, which given my present financial state was a non-starter. As such, whilst in Germany, I decided I needed to get back into regular employment, though if my heart had ruled my head, I may have stayed in Munich.

Northern Ireland took around 400 supporters to the game, inclusive of a charter from the Harbour Bar in Belfast. The atmosphere was naturally excellent, even when I arrived at the railway station to meet Marty and his compadres, who were all decked in green, some five hours prior to kick-off.

It got better when an Irish themed pub was taken over as supporters arrived and congregated.

I have to say I am not happy with the fixation of Northern Ireland supporters meeting up in an Irish themed pub, save for them usually being proximate. I cannot see why supporters who do not want any link with Ireland, however tenuous, would want to patronise a premises adorned with Irish tricolours, road-signs written in Gaelic, and 'travelling' student type bar staff with Irish accents. I certainly don't and 'ban' (unofficially) anyone travelling with me from using them, more because I do not like the 'plastic' atmosphere that goes with them. If I am in Sofia, give me a Bulgarian pub, in Tallinn, an Estonian one and so on.

Inside the said Irish pub, I met a guy called Robert Hunter, who was very amenable and suggested he would like to travel to Kiev the following spring. We exchanged phone numbers, but unfortunately, he got so pissed he exchanged keep sakes with some German supporters, changing a key ring, complete with house and car keys for a small German car pennant.

He didn't swap his match ticket, and good job too as Northern Ireland gained an excellent 1-1 draw.

It seemed to become a trait of Northern Ireland, that they could raise their game against far superior opposition, as on this occasion, and against Portugal the previous autumn and Spain in 2003 (0-0).

Indeed against Germany, Gerry Taggart actually gave Northern Ireland a brief lead before the Germans got their act together and equalised. Then goalkeeper Tommy Wright, a quality keeper who had played for Newcastle and Manchester City in the top flight, proved inspired as he somehow, courtesy of posts heads and various limbs, managed to keep the Germans at bay.

I took the late train back to Munich feeling very contented, looking forward to a night in the bier halls.

Munich's main pedestrian shopping street, Marianstrasse, which passes the main cathedral that appears on all the postcards, is alive at night as the mall has a peculiar mix of kellers, stores, and fast food outlets. It also has numerous sex shops and peep shows and on my way to check out the local hostelries, saw what is, to date, the worst job I have ever seen.

At around 11p.m., an old 'oriental' type male almost collided into me carrying a mop and bucket. Slightly shocked, I stopped and watched about his business: an annoying trait I have, which comes from keeping my eyes on people, and their behaviour, in pubs. I noticed he was going into some peep show booths and he opened all the private screens and began to slop out the floors to clean up all the days' tissues and fluids. Save to say, I did not offer any assistance and continued on my way.

I found a bar, which was advertising an Evander Holyfield v Mike Tyson, heavyweight boxing fight.

However, I did not get to see the fight, instead I was awe struck when a German female, with incredibly harsh blue eyes attempted to talk to me at the bar. It was tough, as I speak English and pigeon French, and Daniella spoke German and Russian. So, the communication was moderate at best, but more likely hopeless although we did spend the night together and had an on/off casual relationship over the next two years.

I am no agony aunt, but have to say long distance relationships do not work, as I never got to know Daniella, except between the sheets. There were no special moments, I personally felt cheap and, with the language making life even tougher, communication to establish likes and dislikes were non-existent. Of course, I would say all this was a pity, but the flip side was, I wasted two years of my life barking up this alley. Never mind: we are all wise after.

Still on the personal theme, late November brought an up-turn in work fortunes, with a new job offered in central London; which I took. It was not an ideal appointment; working at a student residence in Regent's Park, but it served a financial purpose in regards of getting to football internationals. Some cheap accommodation, which came with the job, also helped the financial situation.

1997 AND ALL THAT

It needed to, because following a weekend sojourn in mid-December to Belfast to watch Northern Ireland comfortably beat Albania 2-0, I noted in a so-called 'trashy' Sunday scandal paper a paragraph suggesting Northern Ireland were likely to play a friendly against Italy in mid January.

I tried to get confirmation between Christmas and New Year from the IFA offices in Belfast, but a receptionist said on at least two occasions there was no one to confirm or deny the rumour.

Eventually, I spoke to the press officer, John Quinn, who confirmed Northern Ireland was to play in Italy on (Wednesday) 22nd January.

International football fixtures are a rarity in January in Europe simply because most of the continent is frozen and there is no sanctioned fixture date. However, Italy were in the same World Cup qualifying group as England, and had a crunch fixture against the English at Wembley in February: a rarity in itself, as that fixture slot is almost exclusively a friendly date, often incorporating warm weather training in Malta or Cyprus. Hence it stood to reason that the Italians wanted a friendly match against British style opposition prior to this game and hopefully give the Tifosi (Italian supporters) a moral boosting victory.

Being a large and diverse country geographically, Italy choose not play their home fixtures in the same place, and apparently are duty bound to take matches to the hinterland islands of Sardinia and Sicily. On this occasion, Sicily and its capital Palermo were to play host.

When a friendly like this comes up at reasonably short notice (3 weeks), the scenario was to book a few days holiday and get down to the travel agents looking for a flight bargain. Though the internet now plays a major part, in 1997, you were at the mercy of travel agents and flag carrying airlines as they had this rule that flights were phone number prices unless you stayed on a Saturday night or spent three days holidaying midweek. The cost of a return flight to Palermo with AlItalia was quoted at £722. (Yet in 2004 Ryanair run flights for 10% of that price!). I needed a plan B and quick.

I went brochure hunting around the travel agents in Tottenham Court Road and hit upon a specialist who did short breaks to Sicily. However, it only covered the tourist spots near Mount Etna, and on contact was struggling to find me a hotel that was open in January. It appeared hoteliers holidayed or repaired after Christmas.

Eventually, a hotel was found and I parted with £400 for a four-day inclusive package, staying in Taormina, an idyllic hill top retreat near Sicily's second city, Catania.

Having arrived at the place, I could fully appreciate why sun-seekers travel to places like The Azores in January for a holiday. I am not a sun worshipper but the idea of warm winter sunshine and an escape from coats and scarves and the depression of a British winter suddenly appealed.

Match wise, I had to work out how to cross the island to Palermo using public transport. The trains looked worse than Britain's shambolic set-up, so the options were bus or hire car. I chose the former; deciding to seek a hotel for the Wednesday and left complete with Marty's flag.

Given the short notice of the fixture, Marty who is a flight control officer, then based at Leuchars in Scotland, could not go, but requested I take his flag for display on the pitch perimeter. This duly arrived, in pristine condition, emblazoned with Newcastle (County Down), and diligently made by his Finnish wife Marita. (Flags especially from UK supporters are seemingly very popular, particularly with a town on, presumably as they can be identified by home town supporters watching the match at home)

Missing a photo opportunity with former AC Milan and ex-national team manager Arrigo Saachi, who had recently been replaced by goalkeeping legend Dino Zoff, I did as requested and placed this flag on the barriers around the apex of the corner flag. I was annoyed about this because my Dad had always told me, and the rest of his siblings, to associate yourself with history makers if you got an opportunity. Therefore my schoolboy hero was Fylde international rugby captain Bill Beaumont whom was very approachable, but latterly I have not missed photo opportunities with the likes of ex Dutch manager Louis Van Gaal, and cricketer Curtly Ambrose who was in a queue at St.John's airport in Antigua in 2004. Robert Walsh was gob-smacked I knew who this 6ft 10 inch tall guy was, but I explained myself, giving details of his legalised brutality towards England's cricketers in the early 90s.

Returning to the game, Marty had found a way of watching the match and the flag at home, via satellite courtesy of Italian national broadcaster RAI. Unfortunately, what I didn't know was that countless Italian school children with flares were prepared to welcome the teams onto the pitch and were not too bothered where they discarded them. Of course, one bit into Marty's flag and cut a rather large swathe into it, simply taking the AST out of Newcastle. Shall I say that when Marty received his flag on return it was not long before the tom-toms were beating a noisy bang to Regent's Park! I did try to placate him by saying I had gone to great lengths to steal the BBC's Ray Stubbs' team sheet, ignoring England manager Glenn Hoddle in the process, but this seemed to have little effect.

Northern Ireland lost the game 2-0, giving the Italians a satisfactory training run in the process, especially on the attacking front, as Northern Ireland from memory spent most of the game on the defensive. I remember Northern Ireland having only one serious shot on goal and got a round of applause when I cheered the ball towards the net, as I was literally alone amongst a whole stand of Italians. They also applauded when I diligently sang the national anthem on my own: a theme which was to happen twice more during the year, but thankfully is now a thing of the past as at least fifty supporters now regularly travel abroad.

On retrieving the controversial flag I bumped into a group of IFA officials who compounded my opinion that I was the only supporter in Palermo by saying 'Hey! There's a Northern Ireland supporter'. We chatted about the quick arrangement of the fixture and future fixtures in 1997. The IFA bods were lamenting how difficult it was to communicate with Ukrainian and Armenian officials; teams whom Northern Ireland were to play in the spring, and an opinion I supplanted particularly with regard to travel to Armenia. Indeed six years later, West End Travel boss David Segal and IFA head of international football David Currie were still having problems entering the Ukraine: being turned away from the Ukrainian Embassy in London. The IFA officials also let slip that they were probably going to charter an airline to both countries given the difficulty of standard airline travel.

I was still worried about the logistics of travelling to Armenia, but had recently sealed the flight and accommodation for the trip to Ukraine of which details will follow, but in the meantime Northern Ireland were due to play twice in Belfast before visiting Kiev.

A DIFFERENT PERSPECTIVE

I previously mentioned an all-important match for England in early February at Wembley and still being a member of the England Member's Club, I was entitled to four tickets. However, the previous evening Northern Ireland was to play a more functional friendly against Belgium.

Gavin had organised a great couple of days with the said match in Belfast, flights over for the England game and then a visit to the House of Commons and Prime Minister's Question Time, as the guest of Strangford M.P., John (now Lord) Taylor.

First things first: Northern Ireland totally outplayed the Belgians for a 3-0 victory, featuring a hot shot from James Quinn and a debut for Jeff Whitley who was the first coloured player to don Northern Ireland green.

(Italy beat England 1-0, and the 'lame-duck' Conservative PM decisively beat the heir apparent Tony Blair across the dispatch box, after which we were royally, entertained in the lobby bar by John Taylor.)

Harry Simpson's ticket holders watched this game from the North Stand, rather than the usual seats in the South Stand in front of the press box. It seemed to be cold and unforgiving over there as the prevailing wind blew harshly and the experiment in perspective was quickly dumped in time for the next home game against Portugal in March. The South Stand at Windsor Park seems homely in comparison, with a lot of things always going on. The press doing their bit, the shuffle of the players and staff in the dugouts close by, and the IFA staff with whom you speak on the phone regularly wandering up and down the stand, can give more entertainment than twenty-two players chasing after a ball.

I met up with Robert Hunter prior to the game, and all the talk was naturally about the trip to Ukraine.

We had turned to Gunnell Travel, whom I used for the Latvia trip, and latterly for a personal holiday to Finland and Lithuania (which was an attempt at an escape from the British heat wave that year but failed as the Baltic was similarly enveloped in heat). Owner Terrence Billing was surprised that anyone wanted to go to Ukraine for a holiday and explained that he had not even sent a businessman there for eighteen months, but it did not stop him from taking £600 from us, whilst explaining about fraudulent taxi drivers and career robbers.

Prior to departure, our main concern was visa application, because the Ukrainians would not (and still will not) accept visitors who have no address, and Terrence could not book a hotel more than a month in advance. We were worried, but eventually it all got sorted, but only with a few days to spare, as the embassy seemed to deliberately drag their feet. With hindsight, this is just the Ukrainian way.

On returning to London, I not only had this, the Italy v England game, but the Armenia nightmare to work on.

There was no way I could afford a week off work or an £1,100 airfare to Armenia, but I eventually had a night time brainwave.

When you work in pubs and clubs, late night work can get intense and the wind down afterwards often incorporates watching late night television, which offers very little stimulation. Hence your mind, whilst still active after a hard night's work wanders, in my case to squaring travel circles.

I had somehow dragged up the memory of an off-the-cuff chat with the IFA officials in Italy and the notion that they were chartering an aircraft to Armenia. The day after, I went to West End Travel's office in Oxford Street and announced I wanted to speak to David Segal. Thankfully David gave me the time of day and initially gave me the answer I did not want, in that the IFA were not going to take supporters, as there had been drunkenness amongst supporters on a flight to Albania in 1993 and it was not in keeping to have this risk, as a national team were travelling to do a job. Determinedly, I pressed my case, which was little more than I was a forlorn supporter wanting a thrill. David, now sitting behind his desk began to think and asked if I still worked in catering to which I replied, 'Yes'.

He said he had a meeting with IFA officials the following week and he knew food and a chef were being taken, but was not sure if any other 'staff' behind the scenes were required. He concluded that if they were taking staff he would fight my case as long as I paid my way and did not go overtly as a supporter.

The wait of a week before I heard the outcome was agonising, but all was worthwhile as I was told I would be allowed on the charter, as long as I helped the chef, kept in the background, and 'behaved myself'. Behave myself: I would have stayed mute if I had the chance to get to Armenia!

First though, I (we) had to get to Ukraine and in my case, via an Easter Saturday visit to Belfast for the Portugal game.

PINK PLASTIC MINISKIRTS AND ALL THAT

Northern Ireland drew 0-0 with Portugal on Easter Saturday, but my attention was way-laid somewhat by the trip the following Monday. We had finally got the travel details flying via Vienna and staying in the Republic Hotel in the centre of Kiev, and left for Heathrow with visas in hand.

The arrival at Borispol airport was tempered by sheer fact. I had heard that the arrivals hall was littered with taxi drivers hustling for business, many of whom were hoods who could well charge you $100 for the cab ride to Kiev, if you actually got to the destination. Tales abounded of tourists being robbed and left in the forests and bearing this in mind, Robert and I were somewhat relieved to see a legitimate bus operation taking passengers to and from the front door of respective hotels.

Arriving at the Republic Hotel, it was if we were in Poland ('91), Albania ('93) or Moldova ('99) in that the hotel was exactly the same design in that it had an entry and reception, a mezzanine bar and dining area and a nightclub, aka a brothel, in the basement. Robert looked worried at the standard of the hotel, which was functional at best and certainly not worth £31 a night we had paid, and I tried to reassure him saying that we were a couple and could watch each other's backs. His worries were though confirmed three minutes after we entered the room as there was a knock at the door, and on opening I was asked by two women if there were any services they could (happily) offer.

In Hilton hotels, to which I have become accustomed since my present girlfriend Rebecca has discounted rates as an employee, this is a regular occurrence as the concierge delivers fresh fruit and travel information. However, they do not tend to wear pink PVC hot pants and lace Basques, complete with heavy black eye make-up and red lipstick, as was the case in Kiev.

We quickly found out that the coffee bar manager, in cahoots with the reception staff, was running the hotel prostitute operation. This was because on the first evening we had been out on the town and ended up in a small bar across the street from the hotel and asked two local ladies, who did not seem to be hookers, if they would like a night cap! In pigeon English, they explained that they were banned from the hotel as they were not the manager's girls. I deduced, maybe wrongly, that every female in Kiev was on the game, as the lure of the silver dollar was too much to refuse given the relative poverty of the Ukrainians, with £50 for a nights work feeding a family for weeks. The coffee bar manager also made it quite clear that if you patronised the premises late at night you were expected to avail yourself of his girls. We did not and ended up securing our room with a hefty chest of drawers just in case a late 'security' visit was in the offing.

Things were little better the following morning with brown water flowing freely from the taps and showers and if breakfast was your bag; you had to like peppered eggs and mouldy apples!

A visit to the impressive Olympic Stadium ground ensued after a second more accommodating breakfast experience, to buy match tickets and look at the pitch itself. In most countries abroad, it always seems people can easily access the match grounds and a photo opportunity ensued in the goals, as military conscripts swept the stadium seating area with witch's brooms.

The pitch had not wintered well, to say the least, and was bare of grass in many areas: a fact which seemed to dishearten manager Bryan Hamilton, when we bumped into the Northern Ireland party in their hotel later in the day. President Jim Boyce asked how our hotel was, and his later offer of shower facilities was only narrowly turned down, given the state of our room.

As for the game, Northern Ireland lost narrowly 2-1, and with it any chance of qualifying for the finals in France, but the game was played in front of some 80,000 people who provided a fantastic atmosphere. It was not so great after 15 minutes when the referee gave Northern Ireland a penalty, which I claimed on my own for a foul. Ian Dowie duly scored, which was due notice for me and Robert to get pelted with sunflower seed pips and a genuine worry for our safety overcame the euphoria of the goal. Immediately, the older members of the crowd around us reined in the exuberance of the less pleasant elements, but safety wise I was quite glad Northern Ireland lost 2-1.

At the airport, we met the Irish party, who were flying home via Frankfurt, whilst we went via Vienna, and I got the chance to ask Bryan Hamilton what Armenian capital Yerevan was like. His retort was 'Grim!'

OUTPOST ARMENIA

One of the 'deals' regarding Armenia was that my passport had to be on David Segal's desk on the Friday after we returned from Kiev. The next time, I would see it was when the party rendezvoused at Stansted airport on Tuesday 29th April. I remember that day well because the day before a guy with whom I worked came in the bar and asked what I was doing with my time off for the week. Rather than saying I would be shopping, ironing and the like on the proceeding Tuesday and Wednesday, I said, in front of numerous others, 'I am just nipping to Armenia for a couple of days to watch a football international.' The looks were interesting to say the least, as were those of the air hostesses, when chef Tom Nesbitt, carried a box of eggs, wrapped in cotton wool onto the plane.

Not missing the chance of an autographed football as all the team were in the same plane cabin, I then spent the next five hours contemplating what Bryan Hamilton's 'grimness' really meant and what the kitchen, I was to occupy with Tom for the next 24 hours was like. Surely, it could not have been as bad as Tirana with chip fryer fat akin to gearbox oil, vegetables being recycled off plates, and potash ovens. I (and Tom) needn't have bothered, as the Hotel Yerevan kitchen was full of plates and utensils, and staff, who were keen to volunteer help. Tom would not take risks though and we provided meat and pasta cooked with, and on plates washed in, our own water.

Breakfast and lunch the following day were done in similar fashion as Tom even insisted I slice cucumber with our own knives. Latterly, as lunch had been served, the plane's captain asked what food we were taking home, as he needed to prepare his paperwork to spread the load in the hold. Tom told me to tell the captain, nothing save a few baskets of fruit was going home. As we emptied the food caskets, all the kitchen operatives and restaurant staff began to circulate and the staff were placing vacuum packed steaks by the half dozen into their lockers.

Given my 'job', I had little time for sightseeing, but could not help but see the poverty in which the locals lived, and their dishevelled state of clothing, save some of the more affluent females with the ubiquitous leather mini skirts, gold hosiery, and bright red lipstick. I did agree with Bryan Hamilton's mentioned summary, and the housing in particular was dreadful, comprising mostly of featureless Stalinist tenements. Despite their poverty, the locals were also very friendly: one person seemingly being so happy to see a foreigner that he gave me his Soviet military medals! I later found out, prosperity in Armenia is judged by owning either a shop or more likely some other kind of capitalist operation, most often a simple stall. In one case, on the coach journey to the airport I was shocked to see petrol station staff measure their wares into buckets and then transfer it into car petrol tanks. All to eek out a living!

We departed the hotel, with the (party's) baggage, placed onto an army truck, and humans placed on coaches. We went to the ground: heaven knows where the baggage went. I had spent any spare social time in Yerevan, mostly in the company of academic John Williams, who was researching a book on sport in post-Soviet republics and Alan Smyth who was doing some community work for the IFA. John had taken me to the (closed) Armenian Olympic Association and I reminisced about the amount of his books I read whilst reading Sports Studies at university. We kept the social theme going by having a few pre-match drinks at an impromptu 'general store' type stall in the ground.

The term 'general store' is important in context, because as well as selling beer, soft drinks and hot sausages:

popcorn and (novelty metal) trumpets, yes trumpets, were on sale. They cost a dollar each and I could not resist, though it did not go down well with the crowd during the game, as I ceaselessly tried to get a note out of it. Eventually, the bland huff did turn into a single note, much to everyone's relief as the ten rows either side, clapped as one. They and I had little else to clap about, as the game became a cliché 0-0 draw.

No matter to me if Northern Ireland had got beat 3-0. Sure I would have been disappointed, but I had done it. I had got to Armenia, catering skills and all, and this outpost of UEFA had been breached, at a fraction of the £1100 I had been quoted.

It needed to be, as I found out Northern Ireland had finally confirmed a Far East friendly against Thailand.

15

BET I DO

Soon after I returned from Yerevan, Hearts supporter Scott Allison, who was the head chef of the International Students' House, suggested I might have been to Armenia, but was unlikely to go to the next Northern Ireland game. The 'Fat Controller', as he was nicknamed, soon lost his smirk when I said it was all sorted.

I had been in contact with IFA Press Officer, John Quinn on occasions prior to the Armenia trip, for at one stage Northern Ireland was due to play full (er) Asian tour, including a fixture against Indonesia. That did not come to pass, but a fixture against Thailand did in mid-May; complete with another massive airline bill, this time to Qantas.

I booked a four-day trip, and have to say it was at least two days too long. Sure, I guess the Thai beaches and islands are as beautiful as the brochures suggest, but Bangkok was like being locked in a tobacco smoke filled sauna. It rained each day at around the same time over lunch, and within five minutes of the thunderstorm passing, the streets were dry again, such was the humidity. Also I am no prude, but I do not like being offered a seven-year-old girl to do with as I wish, by her supposed ten-year-old brother. It really brings home the ways of this unfortunate world, but I am happy to be addicted to watching every Northern Ireland game. Yes, I did go in a brothel bar, which was equally as degrading, with prostitutes filing past the punters carrying their respective number pinned to their bikini top. This inhumanness gave me a perfect excuse to leave. Honest Mum! In fact, the nearest I came to any 'exploits', was a full Thai massage, when a young female literally trod on, twisted and snapped every muscle and ligament in my body. Aching (afterwards) is perhaps the wrong verb!

Similar inhumanity was witnessed when I took a day trip after the match to the death camps on and around the River Kwai. I could not believe the brutality suffered by the prisoners of war, which brought a lump to my throat on many times during this humbling journey, particularly when visiting the impeccably tendered graves. I had no shame in throwing a group of Dutch students off the baize-style grass as they saw fit to picnic in this area.

In hindsight, I also wished my granddad was still alive when I returned from this trip, as I could ask just how he and the Chindit regiment battled in close-by Burma. It is a main regret of my adolescence that I did not ask this proud man, who never seemed to be critical or show enmity towards anyone, just how he and his compatriots survived these conditions. I was exhausted, having been satisfactorily fed and watered, in an afternoon, so heaven knows how anyone took up armed combat out there.

There was little combat in the (very friendly) friendly match between Northern Ireland and Thailand, which had very much of an 'after you Sir' feel to it with very little tackling throughout. The game was delayed whilst the Prime Minister arrived and my personal half-time entertainment was an audience with Jim Boyce and vice-President Ivan Gaskell, whose initial remark was 'What the hell are you doing out here?' It was an easy answer to give, and I am sure I was the only supporter who travelled to this game. Some UK ex-pats lent their support, but I have yet to meet any other supporter who left our fair isles for this occasion. Entertainment wise, they must have been informed, as neither side should have got a score as high as 0, but 0-0 was the result.

BALMY BELFAST AND BEYOND

There is always something surreal about watching football in high summer, whether it is an end of season tournament or a date with the early (British) season international date in mid-August. Somehow, I feel I should be at Lord's sunning myself on the top of the open stands as I do regularly in the summer months; saving the jumpers, coats (and match strips) for the protection against winter storms at football matches.

Nonetheless, balmy mid August 1997 saw a meeting between Germany and Northern Ireland in Belfast. This fixture date is almost exclusively used as a friendly date for the UK countries, because players are still only just recommencing competitive league football and their priorities are getting match fit, and international wise, it is preparation for the dates in early September.

Thus far, the team had struggled in the qualifying series, with only one win and four draws, but theoretically three wins from the final three games could see a route to the play-offs with the prize of final qualification for France the following summer. It was nice to dream, but reality had placed the European champions in front of Northern Ireland. However, reality and the dream met head on for ten glorious minutes that evening because Michael Hughes gave Northern Ireland a 1-0 lead mid-way through the second half. No; reality with bells on returned in the form of Oliver Bierhoff who scored three goals to snuff out home bravery. But at least the weather was nice!

As nice as it had been the morning of the game, when a group of Northern Ireland supporters, courtesy of

Marty's now fast growing and respected fanzine, arranged a match against a set of German supporters based in Hamburg. The day before, Gavin and I had a rather long day and night out, via Northern Ireland Railways, and my appalling football skills were exacerbated by my sweating alcohol throughout the game. I did draw consolation from the fact that most other players were in a similar state of inebriation, but was impressed by some supporters skills; in particular Richard Henry; a main cohort of Marty's in developing the Our Wee Country fanzine on-line. Also a few quid was raised for a special needs school in Northern Ireland and the supporter's team was born. Now more official, complete with strip, Northern Ireland's supporters play 'internationals' against other supporters teams, often presenting an amusing sight for sore eyes, as round bellied, hung over and bespectacled individuals try to live a dream. Personally, I just wish I was better at football, not international class, but competitive, though on this semi-drunken performance, I shall have to keep wishing.

I also wished budget airlines had spread their tentacles further by September (1997), as Northern Ireland had to face Albania in neutral Zurich, because of civil unrest in The Balkans. I was not losing too much sleep about not returning to Tirana, but was struggling to comprehend a £350 airfare, via Amsterdam. 2004 direct fares, for a Northern Ireland v Switzerland friendly, from Heathrow with the more up-market British Airways, were only £140! If nothing else, the Easyjet's of this world have sorted out aviation's flag carrying gangsters, and long may this destruction of blatant profiteering continue!

Now off my soapbox, I had to travel to and from this game with only a single-night stopover because work was hosting a launch party for a new Internet café in a dormant part of the building and a three-line whip on attendance was in operation. As such, I flew out of then fledgling Stansted on the day of the game, watched the teatime international, and then had to get back to Zurich airport by 7 am the following morning for a flight home.

Until 2002, when Northern Ireland played out a goalless draw on my return to Liechtenstein, this was without doubt, the worst Northern Ireland performance I had seen. Laughingly we were lucky to get 0, as a 1-0 loss was recorded, but the meekness of the performance was most disappointing, seemed to cause mutterings amongst the IFA admin team and personally was the closest I have ever come to booing a team I happen to support. That includes dire England cricket performances during the Lloyd /Atherton years of the late 90s, but I will not boo a team, even the opposition, out of both manners and the fact that a team is not bad on purpose. If I had not been there on my own, I am sure strength in numbers would have predominated, with jeers coming from a no-doubt Spartan area of the ground. This was also the day, in my opinion, that Northern Ireland began to consistently decline through the world rankings from around 50th to 124th, when Lawrie Sanchez took over in 2004.

Some games though do go down in history as being bizarre for certain incidents, such as the same piece of national anthem music for both teams (different words) in the Northern Ireland v Liechtenstein games two years previously and this was one of those. In the days prior to the game the world had lost Diana, Princess of Wales and Mother Teresa of Calcutta and a minute's silence was held before the game for both people, with Mother Teresa being of Albanian descent. Quiz question or what!

I WANT A STAMP AS WELL!

Soon after my return from the Germany game in Belfast, I had begun to look at organising my affairs for the last group game in Portugal in October. For mass tourist spots like Lisbon, and Portugal itself, the back pages of the heavy Sunday newspapers can be a good starting point. I noticed an advertisement suggesting 3 nights in a 4 star hotel and return flights for under £200. Gavin Nixon was informed, he expressed an interest, as did his Linfield supporting friend Gary McMichael. Robert Hunter was demanding details, as was Richard Henry. With cheques abounding I was quickly booking a trip for numerous bodies, including Roy Bennett, of the Carrickfergus Silver Band and his spouse Denise. The travel agent, based in Croydon, was overjoyed at their seemingly unexpected business, but wished to close the book at a level ten. I was happy as I knew all the travellers and with females around as well, knew nobody would flare up due to drunkenness.

Latterly, whilst at work, the phone rang and a male introduced himself as John, and said David Currie at the IFA had proffered my phone numbers, as I had allowed, with a view to travelling to Portugal on an organised trip. I managed to get an extra seat off the travel agents, but was a little concerned about John; simply because I, nor anyone else, seemed to know him. Personally, I was glad I did because, John Aiken, as it turned out was a really good travelling companion and has been ever since. One intricacy of John, is that this quiet and pleasant person, whom I often stay with in Belfast due the proximity to public transport, changes into a barracking and noisy cheerleader once the referees whistle starts a game.

On this trip though, John's shouting was the least of my problems, for throughout the trip, the only time all eleven of the party were together was during the match in the Stadium of Light. Robert Hunter never made the outward flight because his flight from Belfast to Gatwick was delayed. I tried to bargain with the check-in staff as Robert arrived shortly prior to the Lisbon departure, but to no avail. Then I had to run for the flight as I could not afford to miss it, as I was carrying the tourists' hotel vouchers and was the only person who knew its name.

On arrival, there was a delay at passport control, because the party demanded the officials get a passport stamp, to validate everybody's passport, whilst I went searching in the arrival hall, with success, for a guy holding a 'Schofield' notice signalling our hotel transfers.

Next, a night out which got out hand, as Gavin, statistician Marshall Gillespie, Richard and I hit the town, culminating in the rendition of numerous national anthems whilst making a nuisance of ourselves in the old town. So much for an unintoxicated trip; the remnants of which I was to feel the following morning.

I had to go to Estoril to get the match tickets and had requested an 8 am call before this night out.

The phone rang and I answered saying my 'thank-you' without opening my eyes, and went stumbling into the bathroom doing my business in similar fashion, for I knew if I opened my eyelids I would suffer a pneumatic style headache. I knew at some point, I had to go for valour and open up, which I did as Robert Hunter started the 'You smell like a brewery' pious stuff, just because he had a missed a night on the drink. Surprisingly, I felt fine; until the moment I opened the curtains and let direct sunlight affect me. Save to say I now knew what it felt like having a javelin impaled in my head.

Small beer though in comparison to Gavin who ultimately ended up in a Lisbon hospital with acute headaches; not I hasten to add due to alcohol, but due to a fluid imbalance.

I was told of the difficulties on returning to the hotel in mid-afternoon, but could do little, as the hotel-accredited doctor was unavailable.

I did receive notice of his hospitalisation during the evening and on match day morning (Saturday) proceeded to the hospital with Robert, in some kind of 'Carry on' farce, looking for a sick Ulsterman with a headache. On arrival, in match strip, as we thought this may carry some weight, we marched through (and over) security and began our search ward by ward. Thankfully, we found him and some three hours later, after pleading his case of full health to anyone who could understand even the slightest bit of English, had him in our possession.

His health collapsed, quite literally, some 24 hours later in the check-in hall, when a recurrence of his problem, led to ourselves being delayed for 36 hours, in and out of hospital, as the rest of the party bode thanks and farewell. At least the insurance got us home 1st class, but it did get me a ticking off at work for unauthorised absence.

My concluding thought was, yes, fun trip, but small groups next time! Hospitals are not my bag anytime. Most of the 'regular' supporters travel in groups for obvious reasons, but after this affair, it compounded my personal view that I should travel alone or with a companion.

As mentioned, the eleven of us did sit in row K; section 29 of the Stadium of Light to watch was Bryan Hamilton's last game at the helm. Expectedly, Portugal won 1-0 and shortly after the Irish F.A. and Bryan Hamilton went their separate ways. Winning only one game in this group was personally unacceptable and I have no doubt the shambles in Zurich led to the demise of Hamilton. He should though be given great credit for augmenting a Northern Ireland Under-21 team, which had blooded numerous players, including all-time leading scorer David Healy, into the senior team.

A NEW DAWN

Therefore late 1997 saw Northern Ireland without a manager and a draw for qualification for the millennium Euro Championships in Holland and Belgium to come.

The draw threw up Germany (again), Turkey, Finland and Moldova: a former Soviet Republic to the East of Romania, with a reputation for grave poverty.

Personally, I was alarmed at the thought of returning to Turkey for a football international. I had been to Izmir on an England trip in 1993, where the Turkish supporters pelted the England with coins, rocks, and anything else throughout the game. In the aftermath, when it was confirmed an England supporter had lost an eye from a missile, Turkey were banned from playing in Izmir, and there had been simmering problems when English club sides had visited Turkey in the fledgling Champions League. This culminated when two Leeds United supporters were murdered in 2000.

On the managerial front, I had spoken to David Currie occasionally about who was being lined up for the job, which suggested the 'suspects' incorporated ex-internationals Jimmy Nicholl, Sammy McIlroy, and Danny Wilson. When therefore, ex-Southampton and England No.2 Lawrie McMenemy, with Joe Jordan and Northern Ireland icon Pat Jennings as back-room support, was appointed, many others and I were surprised.

In the mid-80s, the Republic of Ireland had appointed ex-England centre half Jack Charlton as manager; the raison d'etre being to redevelop the team and create a squad and style of play which, whilst not satisfying to the eye, would make the team competitive. The fact this team either qualified or were close to qualifying for all the final parties from 1988, until Mick McCarthy took over in 1996, was a credit to Jack Charlton who created a team from numerous, at best, (dis) functional parts. I am assuming Northern Ireland, by appointing McMenemy, were attempting something similar, and, as always when a new manager takes over, there was a genuine sense of optimism in the spring of 1998. This was compounded when Northern Ireland won their first two friendlies, both 1-0, against Slovakia and Switzerland respectively.

The group of supporters with whom I sit at Windsor Park in the South Stand used to work together, but had drifted into other offices and areas of work when the insurance companies consolidated in the late 90s. As such, football occasions were a chance to catch-up, chat and drink and be entertained by paying £10 (for the Slovakian and Swiss games) to get into a football match. When the football becomes a bit boring, the group entertain themselves by, for example, barracking the referee's assistant to make the visiting team's manager not go out of the 'controlled' area where they can stand. This occurred at the Swiss game, and the second half of most games is not complete without passing the hat, which incorporates putting a £1 in a collective hat and passing it around those paying. Each time play stops, the hat is passed and at the final whistle the person with the hat wins the sweep, which has included BBC radio commentators who sit a few seats along from us.

However, on the night of the Swiss game, one moment occurred which will be personally unforgettable as it silenced, with merriment, the entire block.

Clarke Gibson, a cynically jovial character, whom I met in Albania, had obviously read the papers around the time of the game because there was a dispute going on over gold found in Swiss banks which had been stolen from Jews by

69

the Nazi's when they cut a swathe through Europe in the 1930s. During a break in play he exclaimed, 'Now why don't you give the Jews their gold back!' The block went silent for two seconds and then erupted in laughter, inclusive of Keith Gillespie's mother who, prior to this, had to suffer barracking of her son's lamentable performance. It was not a great comment, but it was just the time, place and instant which made it amusing.

Returning to football, Northern Ireland's third spring fixture, was as pre-World Cup 'fodder' to a fancied Spanish team in Santander; an idyllic town on Spain's Northern coast which could be considered an Iberian Bournemouth, as it is home to many retired Spanish people.

I had visited the town when Graham Taylor's England lost 1-0 to Spain in 1992 and remembered the wonderful beach and ice cream, to which I am a '…holic'; often eating half a dozen in an afternoon, if abroad and in the mood.

Little seemed to have changed when John and I actually arrived.

It was impossible to get an acceptable airfare to Bilbao for a midweek break and we had no alternative, if flying, but to take a £200 flight to Madrid and then transfer, via a six-hour bus ride, to Santander. Others had taken the two-day ferry hike from Portsmouth to Santander, which was a personal non-starter. I don't do boats!

John Aiken is a reasonably easygoing guy, who is agreeable company in that he tends to enjoy a social drink, but is not too keen on an alcohol-fuelled evening out and therefore there is no issue come bedtime or noisy tourist bedtime parties. Or so I thought!

Not long before the Spain trip, the political parties in Northern Ireland had mostly signed up to what was known as the 'Good Friday Agreement', which would ultimately lead to devolved power-sharing in Ulster. Also the agreement was supposed to supplant paramilitary ceasefires, but in reality guns and bombs were merely replaced by punishment beatings and kneecapping. Nevertheless the citizens of Northern Ireland were to vote, coincidentally the day after the Spain game, on whether this agreement was acceptable. The consensus was to accept, but John supported the 'No' camp, and late the night before the game started a conversation with another supporter, which became a little heated, but in the main jovial, over the whys and wherefores of said agreement.

Having never lived in Northern Ireland, I consider the politics of the province the domain of those resident and left the scene, as the protagonists shared a bottle of scotch.

My next memory was going to the toilet during the night and then waking in the morning, as the curtains had been left open, to scratch a scaly substance off my feet. I thought nothing more of it and watched television, as John slept. Latterly he woke to announce he had cleaned everything up before dawn and apologised if I had been woken. Bemused, I asked if his dream was a bad one, to which he retorted that he could not drink scotch, had been sick on it, had a 'spillage' on the floor of the room, but had cleaned it up prior to the morning. Quickly, I went and showered, as I realised the scale on my feet and hands, as I had scratched them, was John's spillage before he had cleared it. Save to say, it was only John and not the burglars! As an ode to John though, it is always best to get any fluids into the toilet: something I have always just about managed to do, as I have been in a similar disposition, but get 'moving' as soon as my head starts spinning.

I will now return to the topic of football spectating and suggest entry to this game almost did not happen, due to events earlier in the day.

A group of supporters had gone into a bank to exchange money and the cashier had tried to crack a joke, suggesting the tourists were Irish terrorists. Taking up the theme, this group went to a toyshop and bought a set of super soaker style machine gun water pistols. Also Richard Henry had been annoyed that player Steven Lomas had suggested he would rather play golf than play football in early June, as the club season had long been over, and had bought a set of plastic kiddies clubs, which he wanted to present to Lomas.

As such, on entry to the ground, the Spanish police decided the supporters that had guns could not get in. Due diplomacy ensued and entry was allowed, but not before the national anthem was sung in the car park as the band played inside the ground. Post-match, after encircling the team bus, the said golf clubs were presented by Richard to Lomas; complete with heated words and some measure of pushing.

The difference in the teams' world ranking was mirrored by both the result and performance on the pitch. Northern Ireland lost 4-1. Though Northern Ireland briefly held the Spaniards at 1-1, the top ten-ranked team eased away in the second half, and all the enthusiasm of the first two games disappeared at a stroke. Personally, I was even more concerned as Northern Ireland had 'leaked' comprehensively for the first time since I began watching.

Usually, if Northern Ireland lost, it was by an odd goal, but this represented a sea change in that the team was, as they say, 'stuffed'. Regretfully it was a phenomenon that continued for the tenure of McMenemy's management.

ISTANBUL: ANOTHER NOTCH

As mentioned, I was approaching the game against Turkey in September with a lot of worry and trepidation. I just wanted to go to Istanbul, watch the game and get home as soon as possible.

Due to the distance, this was impossible, but a two-day weekend was arranged with a flight arrival via Frankfurt, landing at midnight.

Arriving at the hotel, I thought I would just relax for a while, maybe find a bar near the hotel, have a drink and get good nights sleep. Good nights sleep! Quite how anyone can do that in the Hotel Kent is beyond me, as the local mosque, Turkey being an unofficial Muslim state, began its wailing at 5 am in the morning.

As for having a drink, the back street behind the hotel looked to have a few lights on and tables outside. There, unbelievably in a city of some ten million, was Marty and his crowd having a drink.

Everyone started talking about Casablanca, Humphrey Bogart et al, and '...all the bar's in all the world, you had to walk into this one.' I explained that I was there for the wedding, as a bride arrived at 2 am, resplendent in virginal white dress, to marry her beloved. She certainly was not expecting a kiss off a dozen beer-breathed Northern Ireland supporters.

In daylight, late summer Istanbul was as I expected: hot, sticky, dusty and teeming with people, some of whom had less than good intentions, in that two of Marty's friends twice were almost the victims of pickpockets. However, I can see the attraction to the tourist of this city, which has the bridge over the Bhosphorous, dividing geographical Europe and Asia, the symmetrical beauty of the Blue Mosque, and the claustrophobic, and infinite, street markets.

I was not there as a tourist, but more in a functional capacity; a role with a significant amount of worry that only eased when I saw the area where the Northern Ireland supporters were to be grouped in Galatasary's Ali Sami Yen stadium. We were on the bottom deck of a stand; the upper level of which hung over the lower deck, creating, with fencing at each end, a completely safe environment, as projectiles could not reach us.

As Northern Ireland were comprehensively beaten 3-0, with all the goals coming in the first half hour, there may have been no need to worry about personal safety, but I felt an immense amount of personal relief when I got back to the hotel and keep a low profile until my plane departed at 7 am on Monday morning.

In Belfast, I also tend to keep a low profile, in that I do not publicly wear Northern Ireland strips, save for a scarf inside the Windsor Park ground. I consider this a pity, but see it as discretionary, because some of the less informed see a Northern Ireland shirt as an emblem of unionism and British rule. I do not want to walk into trouble if I can help it, particularly if I am in Belfast alone, and would rather be anonymous than controversial. I will not however, NOT wear a strip on the mainland, where others of the narrowed minded ilk have seen fit to insult, particularly in Luton. I usually retort by ignoring them, or to quote Gavin Nixon, tell them to 'Wise up!' There is little point wasting time explaining things, particularly if someone in the supermarket queue seriously asks you if you are involved in terrorism as occurred in a Watford supermarket, in Easter 2004.

LOOKING EAST AGAIN

The autumn matches were both home games, with Northern Ireland notching up a rare (weekend) competitive victory against Finland, 1-0, in October and drawing 2-2 against Moldova on a wild Wednesday night in November. This was a poor performance and there was no way Northern Ireland should have let their lead slip in the second half. However, travel wise I had already begun to organise the return trip to Moldova the following March.

With trips to the former Eastern Bloc, Austrian Airlines is usually a safe bet when searching for an accommodating airline. However, in 1999 even Austrian did not fly there; with the only airline commuting to the capital, Chisnau, being Romanian flag carrier Tarom. Even then, there was not a daily flight, but a commute between Bucharest on (fortunately) a Tuesday and, returning on a Thursday. Therefore, a week off work was needed to complete the trip, with an airline cost of over £300.

On researching this information, I also found out visas were needed to enter both Romania and Moldova: total cost £85. Furthermore, the only Moldovan embassy in near Europe was in Brussels, which meant a night away in the most boring city in Europe, plus return flight. Cost £100.

The embassy was open for visa issue on Tuesday and Wednesday afternoons, and I duly arrived at 2 pm to get my visa. A genial middle-aged male did the business, and had to ask the reason for the visit. I said in my pigeon French that I was circling the 'tourist' reason and the real reason was to watch football. The official smiled and explained it was not a nice place to visit, with little to do and a lot of dirty street-children, but hoped I enjoyed the trip, as I handed over the cash.

Next job was to find a hotel: again an ordeal in the pre-ubiquitous web site days. There was little alternative, after some detailed research, but to approach Inntourist in London. This was the old-Soviet run travel agency, which meticulously arranged the Red Square and Lenin's tomb, 'we will show you only what we want you to see' Westerner's trips to the Soviet Union in the 80s, and had re-invented itself as offering trips to the old nineteenth century silk routes. Its brochure did suggest hotels could be found in the area in question and the Cosmos was booked for two nights. The hotel voucher cost £182, and the bottom line for this trip was £720, the most expensive single trip to date. It was perhaps therefore unsurprising only 9 supporters came to the Chisnau.

One of those was another Englishman, who contacted me via David Currie, suggesting he wanted to go to Moldova as he had met friends there when England had visited in 1996. Chris Johnson seemed a pleasant enough guy and we remained acquaintances until 2002, when he decided to invite his boss on to a proposed trip to Korea for the World Cup without consulting his travelling companion, which was me.

Save to say, I do not keep company with people like that.

Prior to beginning the Moldovan trip, Northern Ireland had a home fixture against group favourites Germany, who despite their favouritism were a shadow of the team that collected the European Championship from the Queen at Wembley in 1996. The talismanic Klinsmann had retired and the rest of the team were ageing or appearing, as the press would suggest, forming pro or anti Lothar Matteus cliques.

Matteus was a brilliant German playmaker when Germany had been at the height of their powers after winning the 1990 World Cup, but nine years later was in his late 30's, playing in a kind of sweeper / distribution role, and had little physical, but a seemingly large divisive presence.

Nonetheless, Northern Ireland posed little problem to the Germans, who won 3-0 and hardly seemed to get out of second gear, in this, by far the easiest qualifying group.

Easyjet were now running a full shuttle to Belfast, which was great as far as I was concerned, because for a minimum of £25, I could get to watch Northern Ireland, which I considered a negligible expense bearing in mind every game for me was an 'away' game. Time wise however, for those commuting from Belfast and travelling onwards into Europe I was beginning to realise how awkward it could be actually travelling waiting for connections etc. Travelling to and from London as the final destination is simplistic as you get your luggage and the go home. For the likes of Gareth Cornett, George Hoey and Sam, who started their journey from Portadown to Chisnau, this meant travelling by road to Belfast, taking the ferry to Liverpool and then an overnight bus to Victoria coach station, just to get a plane to Romania. Once there, Marty's spirit of adventure took over and rather than taking the air route to Chisnau, a 13 hour train ride was undertaken, complete with service halt to change the train bogeys. All to watch Northern Ireland and then begin the journey home!

Other supporters on this trip were 'Mooncat' Raymond Hill, and Justin, then a 20 year old, from Doagh, who has not missed a Northern Ireland game since this date. I often wish I had started my international journey at that age.

The night before departure Marty stayed over: an event in itself, as his snoring often disturbed my sleep, and his socks and shoes were removed from my flat, for obvious reasons. Therefore the moral here, is do the boy-scouts thing and 'be prepared' with Marty, but on the subject of shoes I had hit upon a new niche, which started in Moldova.

Living in Regent's Park, my nearest shopping gallery was Oxford Street, which has little novelty to it when you HAVE to use it, due to sheer numbers of people. However, on one sojourn I had noticed that a sports shop was selling bright green Adidas (Torsion) trainers, which would almost match the brash green Northern Ireland strip. I purchased them and wore them to every away game for the next four years, gaining many admirers, some who viewed them with incredulity, particularly in Eastern Europe. I don't think Carol Sutcliffe, the personnel manager / secretary at the student's residence, had much time for the trainers though, for she noticed them, along with seven other Northern Ireland shirted supporters, when she was showing a prospective finance manager around the bar. That was her problem, unlike a guy in Rotterdam at the 2002 UEFA Cup Final who offered me 100 Euros for them, or John Cornett, Gareth's brother, who wanted me to buy him a pair in 2000, when he saw them prior to my walking up the Garvaghy Road in Portadown in them. This is the main road, which caused problems in the late 90's, when the Orange Order could not walk up it due to nationalist (and police) objections. I even took these trainers to Australia in 1999 and had them photographed on Bondi Beach, as I won a pub bet, which said I could not fly around the world in a week.

In 2004, they were retired, rather worn out sole wise, to be replaced by a new pair (as I bought two) and a pair of 'Mountain Gear' green boots, which I bought in New York. Mountain Gear produces boots that broadly match American Football teams. The New York Jets play in green and white, and almost exactly match Northern Ireland green. In Belfast, I have had at least a dozen people come and ask where they could get a pair, and people sneaking a view out of the corner of their eye when abroad regularly amuse Robert Walsh. In conclusion, I now consider my green footwear as a personal trademark.

Marty had arranged, via the Internet, a rendezvous at Bucharest airport, with a Romanian national who could act as a guide for the week. This was no bad idea, as reports often suggested Bucharest was somewhat akin to Dodge City, with gangs of children who lived in the underground pipe work, marauding the streets robbing whatever they could just to survive. These rumours were true, and I did see numerous youngsters wandering the streets asking for money on our Thursday night return after the game.

I asked a citizen, with whom I met in Bucharest, why these children were around and she explained that they were the remnants of Ceauceascu's brutal socialist regime, where families were forced to have children they did not want or afford, and quite literally threw them onto the street. If the children did not go to an orphanage, which were more like a mental sanatorium, they ended up in the sewers, and disturbingly are now reported to be producing second-generation children.

Similarly, the open streets were awash with mangy and hungry dogs, which permanently disturb the peace and were thrown into the streets, when Ceauceascu decided to hoard Romanies into the city, as he attempted to create an industrialised society out of agrarian peasants.

Returning to the Monday night arrival, the buzzwords were 'Be careful!' stick together and play it safe. Safety therefore meant eating McDonald's and having a drink in an Irish bar. However, alcohol fuelled valour eventually took us over and we asked the (Irish) bar man where we could have good night out. He suggested the best night was 'Club A' and the taxis were ordered.

On entry, I began an argument with a very burly doorman over the entry, which I decided was £20 in Romanian lei. However, he quickly altered my views without resorting to using his physical presence, when he explained the 000s on the currency, which I miscalculated, eventually making the entry a mere 50p! With lager at 20p, it leaves little to the imagination to think of what state we left the premises in, making three taxi drivers 'race' through Bucharest to our hotel. With hindsight, this was not the best idea; particularly as many of us were hanging out of the windows of battered, unsafe Dacia cars, which were a poor cover version of the 1970's Renault5.

It was also not a good idea to pester the Moldovan Embassy in Bucharest, as the other supporters had to do in order to get entry visas. This incorporated a 2-hour queue and wait, a phenomenon repeated for only slightly less time at the railway station for Marty et al. On explaining this to Ioana, whom I mentioned earlier as the street guide, she explained that stamping bits of paper around offices was a national pastime in Romania, paid many wages and was a communist anachronism.

We went our separate ways to Moldova from there, with Chris and I on the one hour plane ride into what has to be the worst airport I have seen since flying into Tirana. Even Yerevan airport, with its exposed concrete and broken light filaments, which had not been repaired by 2003, was the Langham Hilton in comparison, as passport control was nothing more than a cardboard cupboard and the duty free shop was a table.

The airport journey had the official in Brussels' comment ringing in my ears. Mile after mile of depressing grey and brown featureless tower blocks, with windows patched up with cardboard, wood, or anything else the locals could use to repel the cold, made you feel totally unwelcome. The Hotel Cosmos was of similar design; a mere tower block, with the room windows sealed with gaffer tape to keep out draughts and intermittent running water. What was striking though was the dimness of the light bulbs, which hardly burnt, even in the hotel and compounded my view of earlier, in that the further East you travel into the old Communist empire, the less brightly the lights burned. I latterly explained what I had seen, via voice and photo, to a member of casual staff who I worked with.

Alem Hailu was of Ethiopian descent, and very interesting to talk with, in that her mother was once a secretary to Ethiopian Marxist dictator President Monguista. She (and Alem) was posted to Stalinist North Korea, before seeking refugee status in Sweden after 'escaping' through China and Alem explained the similarity between the tenements shown in Chisnau and Pyongyang. Alem also often said how life in North Korea was based solely on the personality cult of leader Kim-Il-Suk and how he explained life was a permanent struggle in his socialist paradise.

Two oases in this comparable misery that was present day Chisnau were the team hotels and a mafia-style pole dancing club we ended up in late at night. I went to the team hotel, as David Currie had asked if I could help out Tom and his staff in the kitchen and we ended up in the club as Marty's internet friend, Marvin, had found out this was the only place open for a drink after midnight. Being scared was not the word for it, as the place was full of angry black-suited 'security' types guarding the hot panted and Basque clad bar and pole dancing staff. This was certainly not a place to fool around and thankfully nobody did.

The cold light of match day morning detailed the poverty of Moldova, with children continually asking for the sweets we had bought over, old ladies selling what appeared to be their belongings and younger entrepreneurs selling, believe it or not, Sainsbury's carrier bags by the market entrance. What was most distressing to see though were children asking for our empty McDonald's boxes. Heaven knows what they wanted with them, but at little more than £1 for a 'Big-Mac' meal we felt a duty to feed a few of these unfortunates. Nowadays, thanks in the main to Jim Rainey and his role in the 'Amalgamation' Committee of Northern Ireland Supporters' Clubs, charity is both more forthcoming and organised with orphanages and schools in 'poorer' countries benefiting from supporters' generosity.

The match was played in the equally depressing National Stadium, where the lights, even in the toilets (sic) were turned off at half time, and was a forgettable 0-0 draw, though Ian Dowie would always argue otherwise. Dowie had largely played a lone striker role for Northern Ireland over the years, but as he aged, his pace naturally dropped, and he needed a sprinter foil up front. However, on this occasion he was convinced (and probably still is) that he headed a chance over the goal line. It was to no avail though and unfortunate all round, because personally for Dowie, that goal would have made him Northern Ireland's then joint leading all-time scorer with Colin Clarke and Billy Gillespie.

Afterwards, Jim Boyce thanked all the supporters for the efforts we had made in travelling to Moldova, but the most bizarre occurrence was Lawrie McMenemy breaking into gibberish slang when quizzed about the game. Marty asked what he was doing about solving Northern Ireland's problems and McMenemy replied by saying, 'Take some variety, that's the spice of life!' Gibberish? I rest my case.

Thursday brought home time, rather the plane return to Bucharest, and though it will do little for the Moldovan travel industry, I have to say I have never been so relieved to wave goodbye to such a place. With hindsight, I would say relieved should be replaced by 'lucky' or 'fortunate', and I do feel genuinely sorry for the people who live in these conditions. I suggest we let such people migrate and do the jobs in Western society we have become too affluent to be bothered to do, if it helps them get on in life, because in 1999 Moldova was stuck in the poverty trap and it was humbling to see.

DECISION TIME

Football wise, the spring and summer of 1999 was a time when both the late and early (new) season friendlies were going to shape a decision. I was very unhappy with both the style and standard of football Northern Ireland were playing in the lead up to a match against Canada at Windsor Park in April. Gavin was away visiting family in New Zealand; a place for which he has more than a secret hankering, and I stayed in a guest house close to the ground, as John was still living in Ballynahinch with his folks. People mentioned are always asking me if or when I would come and stay, but I am not keen or either imposing or inviting myself around, hence a stay at the Ashrowan guest house. New Zealand was probably about far enough away to hide from this quite awful performance, when a last minute own goal gave Northern Ireland a thoroughly undeserved 1-1 draw.

The game itself was shrouded in an amount of (sceptical) controversy because in February the IFA had pleasure in announcing that world champions France were to visit Windsor Park in August 1999.

Now the IFA usually offered a 'free' ticket to a friendly at Windsor Park to those, like Harry Simpson's group, who had bought a 'season' ticket to a qualifying series of games. This had been due in August 1998, prior to the qualifying series beginning, when Malta was being hosted. However, the horrific events in Omagh, a few days prior to the game, when some 30 people died in the name of a group making a political point over the unification of Ireland, quite rightly put paid to the fixture.

Therefore supporters were 'owed' a friendly and many assumed it would be the French game, but the Canada game came first and counted as the freebie. The conspiracy theorists may have a point in that the tickets for the French game were £25, rather than the usual £10 or £12, and it is accounting sense that everyone paid, but both dates in April and August, had become specific international dates, with Northern Ireland regularly participating.

A fixture which was slid into the international calender, was the Republic of Ireland versus Northern Ireland match in late May. This was arranged as a benefit to the victims of the aforementioned Omagh outrage, but had a distinctly end of season feel about it, with the Republic using it as a training run prior to some European qualifiers the following week, and Northern Ireland fielding a very young team, which had been beset with senior player withdrawals. Again the game was poor in front of a disappointing crowd of some 12,000, but somehow Northern Ireland managed to win 0-1, with a prospective Danny Griffin strike.

Personally, I took a day trip to Dublin, leaving at 7.30 a.m and returning at 6.30p.m, like other Northern Ireland supporters, who numbered around 700, taking trains or coaches from Belfast. John was one of those, making a rare visit to the 'South'; a country he feels he does not wish to patronise, as he feels some of the state institutions may be a front to terrorism. On leaving the ground, we discussed the fact Northern Ireland were now 'double' champions. Champions of Ireland in that the Republic had been beaten, and champions of Britain in that they were (and are) the reigning British champions. When mentioning the latter, the fact the tournament had not been played since 1985 held little water. It is who are the holders, which is significant! John et al went back North, whilst I flew home looking forward to a weekend city break to Sydney, in June, to see the Olympic Stadium, a cricketing summer and a return to Belfast for the early season friendly against France.

By August, thanks in the main to the monotony of the flight home from Australia; I had made another decision in that I was to leave my job in London. I had righted the wrongs in the bars at International Students' House and had become bored and disenchanted with the whole goings on, despite being comfortable financially and living almost rent-free in a Regent's Park address. However, I don't like the 'comfort zone' and am always prepared to take a risk for a new challenge. Also it was clear the Students' House did not want me, as there was continual friction between mine and other departments, and eyes passed across tables and corridors with daggers drawn. Thus, the paths were to divide, when I saw fit, but I was hoping for something new before the end of the year.

It certainly happened quicker than that, when I was offered a management position with a company running wine warehouses in France, coincidentally two days after the French visited Belfast. I had always thought about working abroad, now the reality was less than a month away, but returning to the football front, I was somewhat depressed over what had happened in Belfast.

It seems an odd word to use about football support and probably the wrong one, but 'depressed' often rears its head when a supporters' team, has a bad trot. Depression should really mean something like having your home blown away by a hurricane, or losing loved ones in a non-natural way. Perhaps therefore, being 'miserable' is a better phrase and it is bizarre that staff that I have employed over the years always try to temper these vibes by working more efficiently when they know Northern Ireland (or England previously) have lost. I would not be 'miserable, depressed' or otherwise, if Northern Ireland were losing (or playing) with spirit or gusto, but it seemed the team were, cliché wise, 'going through the motions' and lost 1-0. Even the ground seemingly had a disappointing atmosphere for the game, which was not even full despite hosting the world champions, trophy and all!

So a new job was on the horizon, but was a new hobby? I had decided that if Northern Ireland did not change direction and, in a nutshell, it meant dismissing Lawrie McMenemy, I would cease to watch Northern Ireland play football. I personally could not enjoy the experience anymore. Even the social side was on the wane, because the team was so poor people were similarly disenchanted and resigned to the fact Northern Ireland were going rapidly downhill.

Whenever a team has a bad run of results there are always those who contact radio stations ranting and raving about changing managers. That is possible in club football as a new manager can bring in his own players, galvanise those in the treatment room and inject some vibrancy into the club. Similarly with a large country this can happen on the international front, a main example being Terry Venables both resurrecting the career of, and creating a talisman out of an ageing Peter Beardsley. However, Northern Ireland is a minute country in comparison and there are only small pools of players to choose from, who are often from lower divisions or only on the fringe of first team (Premiership) action. Hence the trick is to develop a team deep in spirit, where the sum is greater than the parts, or attempt to develop a group of young players who lose a number of games, but learn through experience and improve by growing up together. McMenemy seemed to do neither and the autumn results bore that out.

AWFUL AWFUL AUTUMN

First up was a home game against Turkey, where I was happy to guest some Turkish friends, whom I had met in London.

I was introduced by a patron at work to Ahmet, a Turkish restaurateur, who had a 40 couvert eaterie five minutes from work. Often I would visit after work and was grateful to him for both hosting numerous parties I was involved in and for clothing, feeding and employing another acquaintance of mine: one Katarina Bezakova.

She was a nanny to a family in North London and was part of a group of Czech and Slovak students who visited work, for a social occasion. We got talking one night and stayed friends, when one Monday afternoon, she arrived at work and said she was homeless, after leaving her (host) family. I housed her on my floor, but Ahmet, though he did not need to, gave her some kitchen work to tide her over. It was a kind-hearted gesture and he explained, it was in the culture of Turks to help friends, hence the very close-knit communities dotted around London.

Ahmet eventually got his match tickets, as he got some tickets via Leslie at the IFA, but never put his address on the ticket application! He was quite ecstatic, as were the other 300 visiting supporters, after the game as Turkey rolled Northern Ireland 3-0. Not a great motivator for the return against Germany was due in Dortmund the following Wednesday.

I returned to London briefly, before departing for Dortmund, and was beginning to worry about my imminently changing surroundings. I was in the 'comfort zone' in London, had no worries financially, worked broadly when I felt like it, and had everything from central London to international airports literally on my doorstep. I was about to give that up for a foreign country, a company whom I knew little about, and a town in Cherbourg, which was over 3 hours from Paris and in geographical terms, in the middle of nowhere. It was little wonder Jon asked me if I was OK whilst in Dortmund, as my head was no doubt regularly in the clouds.

I flew to Dusseldorf and then took the train to Dortmund, which is a typically functional German city. There are few sights, but everything for 'locals' is available, from a zoo to a central shopping mall serviced by a typically efficient (and integrated) transport system.

Jon, Gavin and Ian, a friend of Gavin's, had arrived in the morning, and on meeting in late afternoon, suggesting the town was 'crap' and there was nothing to do. They were right, the nightlife being similar to Vienna, a few years previously, but without the recital. With hindsight, you cannot expect much to be going on in these cities and towns on a Monday, particularly where the pub is not the main (early) evening attraction. Even the ubiquitous Irish pubs are 'dead' on a Monday in most European cities, even London!

Tuesday incorporated a trip to the Westfhalen Stadium: home of Borussia Dortmund, where the match was to be played. It is different from most European stadia, in that it is a specific football ground and not a 'catch-all' municipal operation with an athletics track on the perimeter. I have a deep personal dislike of these such grounds, because you are miles away from the action, due to said track, and the ground is often atmosphere less, as there is rarely a roof which holds in any spectator noise and atmosphere. It is often rumoured that Borussia's ground is modelled on Glasgow Ranger's Ibrox Park, with four huge 'stand-alone' stands on each side, holding some 80,000 heads at capacity, and all stands proximate to the pitch and without fencing. So close in fact I managed to ask Northern Ireland's defender Mark Williams for his shirt after the game as the players left the pitch after the game. He duly obliged.

One thing the Westfhalen did have in common with other grounds in Europe, is that on non-match days entry to take a picture or do something odd like lying in the goal or sit at the press conference table is possible, as long as it does not disturb anyone. The groundsman seemed happy to oblige our requests; something I know would be met with a flat 'No' if requested at numerous stadiums in England: as occurred when Gavin Nixon and I toured some West Midlands grounds one afternoon.

The evening's entertainment saw a trip to Ludenschied for the Under-21 fixture. The town was within 100 kilometres of Dortmund, which is a UEFA/FIFA requirement for U-21 fixtures, but was tough to get to via public transport and necessitated a complimentary ride in a police car to get us to the ground in time for kick-off. Playing the dumb foreign football supporter can have its merits, but the return home was even more surreal in that it was courtesy of Marty's fish wagon.

Marty had numerous supporters in tow and their transport was private and via hired mini-bus, which doubled as a locals' fish transporter and smelt like it. But the moral is, when you need a ride, never look a gift-horse in the mouth, even if your jeans smell like a trawler's drawers for the rest of the trip.

As for the match, Northern Ireland, not surprisingly lost 4-0, and my memories were that Northern Ireland were totally out of their depth. Yes, I was lucky enough to get Mark Williams top: a great souvenir as the shirts have the game's date embroidered, but after a member of a defence had conceded four goals, I was perhaps even luckier I did not get it rammed down my throat.

A second memory was seeing the class of Lothar Matthaus for one instant, but one that created an everlasting personal memory.

Matthaus was an ageing midfield 'general' player, with an awkward reputation, who had once retired from the German national team, but was brought back into the fold by manager Erich Ribbeck, as a sweeper who could use possession from the penalty area in more constructive way than a prospective 'hoof'. I noticed him place two sixty-yard passes at the toes of his teamates, hence developing superb attacking options. Whether such skills merited a place in the team, as Matthaus contributed little else, is debatable, but it had the said effect on me, if not the home supporters who cared little for Matthaus, as he played for Dortmund's sworn enemies Bayern Munich.

Football wise, the awful autumn continued in October with a 4-1 defeat to Finland in Helsinki on a freezing cold evening in the Olympic Stadium

This, surprisingly, was a very difficult place for me to get to, because I had completed my move to Cherbourg on the Northern coast of France only some three weeks before. Hence, I had to take a train to Paris, borrow a bed off Sarah Pollitt's sister Eleanor for a night, and then fly from Charles de Gaulle to Helsinki.

On a simple map, you would think Cherbourg is not that far away from to South coast of England, or indeed Paris. You could not be more wrong, as it is eight hours from England on a standard ferry and four hours from Paris. This is because the train has to stop at all the tiny villages on the way through Normandy, as the French public services honour their commitment to the local taxpayers.

I did make my 9.30 am. Air France flight to Helsinki, which surprised myself as I got totally lost on the Paris metro whilst attempting to meet Eleanor and almost decided to pack up and get the overnight train back to Cherbourg.

Arriving in a cold autumnal Finland, I went to my hotel and then to the ageing Olympic stadium to get a match ticket. On the approach to the ground I bumped into Paul Duffin and Justin who invited me back to the team hotel, where they were also staying. President Jim Boyce bought everyone a drink and asked manager Lawrie McMenemy to join us. I was glad he didn't, because, as far as I was concerned this guy was ruining my holidays, whilst suggesting in the press he did not need the hassle he was suffering managing Northern Ireland.

At least four times a year, I was travelling off to watch Northern Ireland and was getting no return football wise whatsoever. In Helsinki, where, as mentioned, Northern Ireland were comprehensively beaten, I gained no pleasure from watching the game, particularly as I also had to stand and wait for a bus to the airport at 6.30 am. on the Sunday morning in a bone numbing Helsinki central square.

On the plane back to Paris, I made a decision, which included continuing to visit Belfast for the home games, but to cherry-pick away games (or trips) as I saw fit. For example, I had always wanted to visit Iceland and would do so when the national team were playing a top draw side. In short, the Northern Ireland experience was over, if McMenemy continued to manage Northern Ireland. It seems my decision was personal, and yes, it was. Whether fact or not, it appeared that what had become my personal nemesis was going to continue as Northern Ireland's manager for another two years as he was (supposedly) offered a new two-year contract. There was genuine relief all around the supporters I know, when this was declined and McMenemy resigned. Selfishly, I could also continue attempting to get to each Northern Ireland game.

NEW ERA, NEW DRAW

When speaking to David Currie, from what was becoming a rain soaked wind damaged Cherbourg winter, I naturally asked who was going to take over the reigns. David's comment, as in 1997, was 'the usual suspects', which would include Macclesfield's Sammy McIlroy, a Northern Ireland hero from the early 80s, Jimmy Nicholl, who was Billy Bingham's assistant, and ex-international Danny Wilson, who had been at Sheffield Wednesday. However, it appeared nothing was going to occur manager-wise prior to Christmas, but there was due to be a draw made for qualifying groups for the 2002 World Cup finals in (South) Korea and Japan.

The IFA were disappointed with said draw, because the countries thrown up did not include a 'big-fish', which could provide extra all-important media and corporate revenue. However, I was more than happy to be visiting the Czech Republic, Denmark, Bulgaria, Iceland and Malta, as they were countries I had never visited before, though Northern Ireland were to visit Malta in a March friendly.

Northern Ireland's choice of manager, early in the new millennium, was the obvious one in Sammy McIlroy. He had guided Macclesfield to stable Football League status and was well respected in football circles, as well as being seen as something of the prodigal son returning in Northern Ireland.

In the early 80s, he had been the mainstay of Northern Ireland's midfield, which had qualified for two World Cup finals, been the only country to beat Germany home and away in a qualifying series, and, as mentioned, won the last British Home International Championship. As such, he was a popular choice, who would be given time by supporters to mend what I felt was the shambles left by McMenemy.

The one legacy from the Bryan Hamilton (and McMenemy) era was that he developed an Under-21 squad, which could bleed youngsters into the full squad. Prior to 1998, Northern Ireland did not have such a team; something that Gavin Nixon felt was shameful, but latterly has provided the senior squad with goalkeeper Roy Carroll and midfielders Damien Johnson and Stuart Elliott.

Another player involved in the Under-21 squad was a (then) Manchester United striker David Healy.

McIlroy had no problem playing Healy in his initial match in charge against Luxembourg in February, thereby stamping his personal authority on the team, as Northern Ireland said good-bye to Ian Dowie, who had clearly been struggling for pace during the dying embers of the McMenemy reign. Healy even scored in an expected 3-1 victory against one of the minnows of European football. The Daily Mail reported Northern Ireland had sixteen supporters at the game, which was about right, inclusive of John, who was making a rare foreign sortie. David Currie latterly asked me why the supporters were barracking numerous agents of the Luxembourg team and the match officials. I explained the match was not the greatest spectacle in the world and we turned our attention to the said Luxembourg dignitaries who were continually leaving the neutral area or the match official whose performances left rather a lot to be desired. This phenomenon is a common trait amongst the often-small group of Northern Ireland 'away' supporters who entertain themselves when the football is not satisfactory.

This fixture suited me personally as I could travel across France to the evening match, on a train ticket, which cost only 180Francs (£18) due to rail operator SNCF's (pre-booked) Christmas sale, and then back to Paris for a flight to Manchester to visit my mother's birthday.

The trip home for a few days made me realise two things. Firstly, as intimated, I did not realise how big France was. It has roughly the same population as the UK, yet four times the landmass, and on the motorway or railway, you seemingly go forever, before reaching anything like a large town. From Cherbourg, which in itself is a typical small port town, a la Folkestone, you have to drive some 150km before reaching Bayeaux.

As such, in places like Cherbourg, the town is very enclosed and typically traditional French and is hence very difficult to interact. Few speak English (but I was not expecting the French to be fluent in my tongue), and though there was a small ex-pat community, made up of Cornish building contractors, supplanted by the shop's (regular) customers, who brought papers, crisps and (Cadbury's) chocolate, the emphasis was very much on being lonely.

This was the second characteristic I realised. It is not something I was unused to, as I was used to working and travelling alone and often enjoying the experience of solitude and unilateral decision-making. However, when at 'home', there were always creature comforts as varied as fish and chips and the BBC and save for the radio, there was none of this in Cherbourg. Also work was difficult, as I was in the process of breaking up a very difficult staff cartel via, what I consider, my honest, up-front, management style. I was therefore somewhat relieved when I was offered a different position in Calais, with its proximity to the UK, Paris and the Low Countries.

After two months in Calais in the spring of 2000, I had forgotten the Cherbourg experience, and had even been 'accepted' by the French employees. This was because I had become an 'approachable' deputy manager at the main Calais 'mega' store, who appreciated the views of the staff. The manager, was a Frenchmen called Jean-Michel and nicknamed 'Le petit merde' (Little Shit), who seemingly cared little for anyone save himself or his wife, who was the overt spy, always listening to and watching staff. I accepted that 'workers' stuck together, especially in France, with their peculiar practices that, I incorporated and listened to. Lunch breaks, refusal to work Sundays, 'functionaire' holiday practices, and support for the French lorry drivers, who went on strike for the people of France, not themselves, all became the norm for me: a fully fledged free marketeer. Ultimately, Fabrina, Marie-Aude and Tracey, three of the till girl 'mafia', encouraged me to become fully French and apply for a carte de sejour (staying card), which was the first step to French citizenship. I did this and sure enough it opened a lot of doors in the minefield of French government bureaucracy: to doctors, health insurance and the like.

MALTA WITH THE O.A.P.s

In between moving from Cherbourg to Calais at the end of March, I had to fit in an away trip to a low key friendly cum training camp in Malta.

The French (and European) answer to Thomas Cook is Carlson Waggonlit and the Cherbourg branch gained my custom in early January. My French was improving rapidly, but I was still struggling to make myself understood, though did manage to explain ALL I wanted was a three-day trip to Valletta, not a week-long architectural expedition to all points with a six-feet dig in situ, as I was expected to buy. It appeared city-breaks were not really a great sale option to French tour operators, but eventually an operator was found using Air Malta from Paris-Orly, which is like the Paris Gatwick, offering a four-night trip, leaving on a Sunday evening.

When in France, and travelling to the likes of rugby at Stade du France or an airport, I always wore a Northern Ireland strip, which neatly matched the Adidas Torsion green trainers I had bought for the trip to Moldova in 1999. These quickly became my trademark and I developed the nickname 'diable vert' (green devil), as (French) people often asked me where I had got them from and drew many a glance from passers-by, particularly in Eastern Europe. A similar phenomenon quickly developed in the check-in queue at Orly, but perhaps more probably due to my age, as I must have been thirty years younger than any traveller. It appeared I had been booked on an OAP's sunshine break: to all intents and purposes a Shearing's holiday in the air. The flight arrived at 1 am. and we were transferred to the comfortable looking Castella Valletta hotel, but not without a twenty-minute delay before the plane was parked and a similar delay for luggage.

I have mentioned this because this is a 'Room 101' hate for me, in that a plane lands, takes another age to park up and then there is another interminable wait for luggage; often adding upwards of an hour to your journey time, whilst you are standing around doing nothing.

I was looking forward to a good night's sleep and lie-in after travelling most of the day from Cherbourg, but it did not work out. At precisely 8.30a.m. the phone rang, with a professional sounding French-speaking female offering me my complimentary place on a coach tour around the island. I politely declined and returned to my slumber only for it to be disturbed with a similar phone call half an hour with the same person suggesting the bus was about to leave. My schoolboy French was now more forthright, as I suggested I did not want to go on tour with a load of (French) old biddies.

What I did enjoy though was the warm spring sunshine Malta had to offer, after the continual rain clouds of North West France, with blue sea and the ubiquitous ice-cream parlours. I love ice cream and local cakes and will eat at least half a dozen different ice creams in an afternoon should the mood (and the town) take me. The best ice cream is in Italy and Spain and surprisingly in Ukraine, and for cakes visits to France and Spain and the local corner-shop 'ancien' bakers are a must.

Public transport in Malta is via a yellow bus, and the island appears to be a dumping ground for the world's old buses which literally clank and clatter around what is the world's fourth most populated place. As such, there is little green grass, and I assume that in high summer the place doubles as a dust bowl, complimented with bus delivered diesel fumes.

The match was played on a Tuesday evening at the national Ta' Qali stadium, but prior to that, the Under-21 fixture was played at the home of Hibernians F.C. Surrealness in itself, with supporters hot-footing it around Malta in mini-buses watching Northern Ireland teams play Malta. Northern Ireland won both games: 2-1 for the Under-21s, and 3-0 for the senior team: as straightforward a win as the score line suggests against, at best, moderate opposition.

The Wednesday was a time killing day waiting to go home, wasted by taking boat cruises from St.Julians to Valletta, viewing museums about German occupation and even by-passing the house where actor Oliver Reed left this world. Personally, I do not like days like this, where you merely watch the clock going around, but in places like Malta, there is little else to do save sit by a pool and go drinking. I do not mind the latter, as a night out with Gareth Cornett and the rest of the Portadown supporters on (the final) Wednesday night testified, but cannot sit around in the sunshine! That in essence is what a Maltese holiday is for.

My return to France was, as expected, completed in the company of another large OAP contingent, whom I hoped enjoyed their sojourn around the sights (sic). I didn't, and knew I would be returning within eighteen months, as Northern Ireland had to return in October 2001.

If the trip to Malta was a time consuming affair, then my trip to Belfast a month later for a friendly against Hungary was anything but, as I spent two days travelling to and from the fixture.

Though I had relocated to Calais within days of returning from Malta, I had made arrangements as if I was living in Cherbourg. As such, the logistics meant taking a train to Lille, a further (TGV) train to Paris: a third train to Beauvais, a cab to the airport, a Ryanair flight to Dublin and finally an Ulster bus 'Goldliner' service to Belfast. The same was required to get home to France the day after, but there was little option, but take this route because it was in the days before flag carrying airlines were prepared to take on budget airlines over cost, particularly on weekdays. Air France quoted over £400 to fly to Dublin, yet burgeoning budget carrier Ryanair quoted a return to Beauvais for £140. Though Beauvais is little more than a landing strip in a field and nowhere near Paris (around 60km), the route did serve a purpose.

I met Gavin in The Crown liquor saloon on Victoria Street, opposite the bus station, some two hours before kick-off after travelling some ten hours to Belfast complete with picnic in hand.

Obviously, most people travel with required baggage, but as explained, I hate waiting and had toothpaste and clean socks and pants in my coat pocket and a picnic in a bag.

The ticket master of our little section, Harry Simpson had complained at the last home fixture the previous September, that he was hungry and did not wish to eat what is nicknamed a 'Windsor burger'. These are typical football ground (burger) meals and consist of a griddled cooked mass catering burger sandwiched between two piece of semi-stale and raw burger bun, finally complimented with cremated onions and your choice of sauce. Food not for the faint-hearted or for those with a health conscious mind.

As such, it was suggested I bring a French picnic to the next game, which I duly did, through all the various transport services and including Parma ham sandwiches, chocolate pralines, masses of pistachio nuts, the shells which were still on the floor the following August, and oysters and snails.

The BBC commentary position is within inches of our seats and reporter Peter Slater was gob smacked to see the catering develop during what was a pretty boring game. In fact, the face of David Kirkpatrick, as he ate a snail, was perhaps the most enduring image of the evening, as I spent most of the game battling to open oyster shells. I have to say I like oysters, but there is a time and a place and a cold Windsor Park is not one of them. Nonetheless it did provide a pleasant diversion from a poor game, which Northern Ireland lost 0-1.

CALAIS DIVERSIONS

To quote David Currie, 'Northern Ireland are taking a break from international football': in that following the Hungary game, the senior team were getting not involved in the pre Euro 2000 friendly/team fodder merry go round.

This suited me, as I had arranged a holiday to the said championships in Holland (and Belgium) with Gavin Nixon for ten days and work wise had just been made manager of one of the chain's smaller Calais shops. The premises had a reputation for being a winning fruit machine, in that people often helped themselves to stock without paying, and therefore needed some serious hands-on management. Also, having booked the Dutch holiday, I could neither afford to, nor have time, to take another one.

Whilst re-developing the business, I both needed, for obvious reasons, and became very friendly with David (Charlut), the company stock checker.

David was handy to know in that he only has one eye and can easily drive when he and everyone else is drunk, as he is permanently in 2-D vision. More seriously though, he is a football lover, and suggested we go to a few games. David Currie quickly obliged in that respect by supplying four tickets for the 2000 Champions League Final at the 'local' Stade du France in Paris, where I was astounded to hear he would like to visit Belfast to watch Northern Ireland (and thank David Currie for getting said match tickets).

Over the years, numerous acquaintances had expressed similar intentions, but had backed out or disappeared when a match approached. I found this annoying, because whether it is a fault of mine or not, I always tend to take people at face value, and when a match is on the horizon I at least expected a phone call with someone making an excuse. It is however, not as annoying when people express an interest in travelling abroad to watch football (or holiday). They will always be up for the trip until the cost, or money, is mentioned. Then, Bank of Shaun is expected to kick in and pay for a trips' deposit (or more) on someone else's behalf. Simply, this no longer occurs, because I will announce my travel plans to anyone interested and let them do their own bookings and reservations. This is why it is so easy to travel with the Gavin's, John and Robert Walsh, as we will meet up, probably at an airport, but arrange and pay for our own flights; as we work on the moral that money and friends do not get on.

There were none of these problems with David: the only issue being which game in Belfast to attend. Was it to be the next match; an August friendly fixture against Yugoslavia or a competitive autumn international?

Coincidentally, Gavin Nixon had mentioned that he wanted to visit Wembley in the autumn for an England v Germany international. These two European heavyweights had been drawn together in the World Cup qualifying group and the (English) FA had poignantly decided this fixture, in October, would be an ideal way to draw the twin towered Wembley to a close. As I was still a (dormant) member of the England Travel Club, I was entitled to apply for two tickets, and in short exchanged those for Gavin's Belfast ticket which went to David, who would watch Northern Ireland play Denmark.

Before that fixture though, Northern Ireland were to host the Yugoslavians in mid-August, closely followed by Malta in the opening World Cup Group 3 qualifying game.

Any Yugoslavian fixture bizarrely holds a special place in Northern Ireland, because it was the Yugoslavs who broke the embargo on international football in Belfast in April 1975. Civil unrest had meant no team had visited since USSR in late 1971 and the Ulster football public seemingly do not forget this and the likes of Harry Simpson often mention this game as a (pleasant) watershed in the dark days of 'The Troubles'. During those three odd years in the wilderness, Northern Ireland played at 'home' in places such as Hull and Coventry.

As for myself, the trip to Belfast was sandwiched around a cricketing summer. I was enjoying day-tripping to and from England and in particular Lords and the beautiful Canterbury cricket ground, as England, at last wrestled the initiative from the visiting West Indies, after a thirty year battering from the likes of Malcolm Marshall and Michael Holding. The trips always incorporated a fish supper stop-off in Dover; something which I also enjoyed with Gavin, courtesy of the Friar Tuck chip shop just off the Newtonards Road in East Belfast. This occurred at tea-time on the Tuesday night prior to the game, after Gavin and I had done something which astounded the locals I knew in Portadown: those in the main being the Cornett brothers; Gareth and John.

On arriving in the town we took the car to Drumcree Church, which was known as a unionist flash point, because it makes the start of an Orange Order (July 12th Sunday) march which culminated by a walk up the Garvaghy Road, before a return to the church. The said road is in a nationalist area and in the early 90s, the locals, led by so-called 'community leaders', decided, rightly or wrongly, to make a stand against the Orange Order and halt the marchers, whom they felt were offensive towards their particular tradition and ideals. Obviously, this created considerable civil unrest and made early July, which is the culmination of the (Unionist) marching season, an unpleasant time for many, as both traditions in Ulster stand their respective corners.

Ultimately, a Parades Commission was created to determine whether, and over which route, a march could take place: even encompassing the Belfast Marathon, which one of the Commercial Union's Windsor Park contingent, in David Seeton, helps organise.

On leaving the church, we went into town, parked up, and walked down the Garvaghy Road, resplendent in trademark green trainers. We were greeted at road end by Gareth, whose brother John we had passed earlier, hard at work in the local butcher, and he was shocked by our actions, concluding only 'tourists', like me, and local residents walk up 'that' road. As a Protestant, he certainly would not walk up the Garvaghy Road, even in his job as a postman.

As for the main event the night after, Northern Ireland lost 2-1, in another disappointing affair. It appeared David Kirkpatrick was more interested in watching the Yugoslavians, who had a reputation for fighting (often amongst themselves) than the game, but at least he turned up.

Being staged at the height of the summer holiday season; only some 6,500 bodies attended the game, and this appeared to put a question mark over future international friendlies. Apparently, it costs a minimum of £50,000 to stage a friendly and on an interview on BBC radio, President Jim Boyce a couple of days after the game suggested he was worried about the cost, especially when Windsor Park was not full.

Since terrace standing at internationals was forbidden, Windsor Park has often always struggled for atmosphere as only three sides are occupied, with the Railway Stand (goal end) only holding 300 spectators. A half empty stadium exacerbates the situation and so ensues a vicious circle in that the team is not performing, then people stop coming, the atmosphere is dull, then more stop coming and the team loses the support it needs. Thankfully, this situation was arrested by a favourable 2006 World Cup draw, which saw a scramble for tickets, preceded by the IFA and various supporters bodies generating support, even though the team was failing.

The team did not fail, thankfully, in the September game against Malta, winning 1-0, although at times it was a close run thing as on one occasion a Maltese player missed an almost open goal. Obviously this was the result Northern Ireland wanted, as the idea behind the group strategy, as far as Northern Ireland was concerned, was to start with a home fixture (and a win).

As soon as the game had finished, I was hotfooting it back to London, as I had a cricketing appointment at the (Kennington) Oval the day after, but was looking forward to the next fixture, as David would be in tow.

David was different from many French people in that he was not 'enclosed'. The French are fortunate in that they have glorious beaches, the Alps and Pyrenees, incredible scenery and a pleasant climate within their borders. Therefore there is not a great necessity for the French, who see it as important to support their own (tourist) industry, to travel externally. Having both an English mother, and grown up in Madagascar, David had travelled extensively, but not to the island of Ireland. As such, we arranged a full weekend away, including a Friday night in Dublin; a train transfer through the rugged and autumnal Mourne Mountains to Belfast and two nights in respective Irish guesthouses.

I had been to the Champions League final in Paris and a couple of European Nations games in Brussels with David and as such he had only been in first class stadiums to watch internationals. I had explained that Windsor Park was merely a ageing club ground used for internationals and not to expect much, off the pitch at any rate. On the pitch I was fully expecting, tongue in cheek, Northern Ireland to win 7-0! Of course, that would not happen, but a David Healy pile driver did shock David, as I explained this always happened at Northern Ireland games! (Not).

The Healy goal was as significant as it was brilliant as it beat Manchester United and Denmark icon Peter Schmeichel. In the match build-up Schmeichel had been asked if he knew Healy, as he had been at the same club in Manchester United for a while. Schmeichel suggested he did not know him personally, but certainly did following the game, which incidentally courted controversy as Danish company Danepak sponsored it, and not an Ulster farming concern.

Latterly the Danes equalised in slightly controversial circumstances, but a 1-1 draw would always be seen as satisfactory against a very functional Danish side, which always qualify for final events, but are never considered favourites.

After the game, David wanted to see a few 'sights', which included the intricate street murals and the respective bunting and flags flying off the lampposts, as well as the internal antique beauty of The Crown liquor saloon, complete with web cam, which he used to 'wave' back to Calais.

Naturally I asked David what he thought of Belfast, soon after we had seen four men fighting on a Lisburn Road street corner, but before we went in to Robinson's on Victoria Street. He was typically diplomatic, suggesting 'It was OK', but I guess the night was better than that as we left Robinson's with two ladies in tow.

I was single at the time, and therefore answerable to nobody, but David wasn't and spent the night with an Australian lady called Kath. I worked with his girlfriend/live-in partner Stephanie and in the cold light of the train journey back to Dublin naturally asked what I/we were going to do. I happened to like working with Stephanie and was, of course, friends with both, but I was surely going to become very uncomfortable. David told me to leave things to him and it would be sorted out by the time I got back from Iceland, which was the next port of call on my weeks' holiday.

True to his word, it was, as David went out front and told Stephanie what had occurred. Sure she was upset, but it did not harm our working relationship and I did not know David and Stephanie had not been getting on for a while, but had merely been existing together. Ultimately all ended up well between them as David broke his shackles and fell in love with Tracey, a Cobh-born Irishwoman woman who lived in Cherbourg, whom he ultimately married in Rome on a stinking hot Friday in July 2003. As for Stephanie, she moved to Paris and fell in love with a young Frenchmen: both of whom were more than hospitable when I visited Paris for rugby internationals. As for me, I was glad what could have been a very sticky situation turned out well and a trip to Belfast was actually responsible for at least one person's future happiness.

A WISH COMES TRUE

As I mentioned, the second part of this international double header, was a trip to Iceland; a country I always had at the head of my visiting wish list.

David and I took the plane back to Beauvais and I spent the night in Paris whilst he took the no doubt 'thoughtful' road to back Calais.

By 4p.m. the day after I had arrived in Iceland at Keflavik airport; complete with duty free shop on entry. This is simply because the price of a bottle of drink is extortionate, and as I found out when I began visiting Denmark in 2001, best practice is to bring friends a bottle of scotch as a house present. Prices in the government controlled bottle stores begin at £30 for a bottle of vodka and such is the society's view on alcohol, that all the bars have darkened windows, comparable to old-fashioned bookmakers and sex shop windows in the UK. In short, drinking is deemed an adult vice.

The airport is situated on what could be forgiven as a lunar landscape, but this is just Icelandic scenery, bereft of trees and greenery, but strangely beautiful in its own way as the harsh autumn sky hit the rocky outcrops on the horizon. It is also the place where many car advertisements are filmed.

I was sharing a hotel room at the SAS Radisson with Gavin Nixon, who was celebrating his birthday by visiting Iceland and had arrived he day before, via a London flight. He had met up with the Portadown mob and Marty's party and they had hired people carriers for the day to visit the geysers and ice shelves in the Icelandic interior. They had also stumbled across a student venue in down town Reykjavik, selling half litres of lager at a more than competitive £4.

Temperature wise it was literally freezing; a far cry from the mild, café cultured autumnal Paris I had enjoyed only some 24 hours earlier. It was the first week of October and I had four layers of clothes on as I watched the Under-21 team play in a park in the Hafnafjordour sports park. I can accept that, as I am used to the cold, but found the air I was breathing painful.

In Liechtenstein I had noted the air pained my lungs, as the mountain air was clean and thin. This was a similar experience but was salt filled due to the proximity of the sea and was painful as inhalation reached its peak. It did not stop us playing football across a motorway though after the Under-21's game finished, complete with some supporters wearing their sombrero's; a piece of kit designed to mock the freezing conditions.

It was still freezing throughout the following (match) day, as I even sought solace in a shopping mall near the hotel prior to the game. Some sought similar respite in a lap dancing bar, but all the supporters seemed to meet in a fish and chip shop on a street corner near the bus station in the town centre. As an amateur fish and chip aficionado, I have to say this place sold the best battered cod I have ever tasted and it even ran out on match day.

Now living in France, I had decided to bring a 'supporters' flag along, but took a different tack in that I bought a French 'bleu, blanc, rouge' along with an apt and relevant slogan which may get some television coverage, if the supporters were in the place opposite the cameras. I had decided to put 'Calais-Scrap the Euro' on the flag, sending a message to those who felt it was a good idea to lock themselves into a single currency.

The French government had enthusiastically signed up to the project and the currency value had collapsed in the summer, meaning the French people had seen the value of their currency, (which was physically still the Franc), and pensions collapse. Also they were worried that they may have to declare their actual wealth when they cashed in their Francs for Euros, as many French had the tradition of storing their money in so-called 'Marie-Curies' (500FF or £50 notes) under the mattress. As an aside, the Euro juggernaut did not stop and was launched amid great fanfare in 2002, but the only two countries ever to have a referendum on the subject, Denmark and Sweden, both said no thanks. Enough said!

The flag was resplendent on television, as pictures were taken live by BBC Northern Ireland, but the team succumbed to an embarrassing 0-1 loss. Jim McComish, sought out Sammy McIlroy after the game, suggesting he had spent a lot of money watching 'that shit', to which McIlroy explained bluntly that the team did not lose on purpose. He was right, but the consequences of this loss were dire, as it would probably mean Northern Ireland would now not qualify for a trip to South Korea or Japan.

When a qualifying series starts a supporter always hopes for the best even though with teams like Northern Ireland there is little chance of qualifying. However, after a win and a draw, the latter against superior opposition, personal optimism did abound, but this defeat brought back a cold sense of reality. It was such a pity, no disaster, because three points from this game would have had Northern Ireland at least in the group melting pot as the group went into winter hibernation.

As for the rest of the holiday, a trip to the Blue Lagoon was in the offing. This is an open geothermal pool and is akin to a massive natural hot tub. Locals believe the silt on the lagoon floor is a healing agent if rubbed on the skin and true to form many were bathing themselves in this hot silt. As for Gavin, and me we were told not to drink a bottle of French wine in the pool and latterly took off for what else, but fish and chips!

UNWANTED COVERAGE

The Iceland game was the last of the year, with Northern Ireland deciding against a November international, but pencilling in the Norwegians for a Windsor Park visit in late February 2001.

Such a fixture made common sense, as Northern Ireland had two Scandinavian countries in the qualifying group and Norway, naturally closed off from home fixtures due to climate, would need a friendly in Northern Europe to ensure its large contingent of English players could easily commute to join up with the squad. Northern Ireland's weather would also more likely guarantee any harsh climatic conditions would be avoided and the fixture would be honoured.

This however, was in question when I got to Luton Airport on the morning of the fixture, with snow on the ground and air thick with frost.

I had taken to travelling to home games via night time ferries and a train from Dover at 4.45a.m., so as to be at Luton for a 10.30a.m. flight, but on this occasion made a phone call to Lesley at the IFA to see if I should actually check in. An affirmative was given and ultimately we arrived at Windsor Park in nothing less than Arctic conditions. However, events off the pitch grabbed the headlines more than those on it, as Northern Ireland lost 0-4.

I have tried to keep politics and sectarian issues to a minimum in these memoirs thus far, but at this game they reared their head big time; circling around Celtic player Neil Lennon.

Lennon had first come to international attention with a combative midfield display against Portugal in Porto in 1995, whilst plying his club trade for Crewe Alexandra. His talent saw him graduate to Leicester City and when his club manager Martin O'Neill left for Glasgow Celtic, Lennon soon followed him. International football wise, this was perhaps not in his best interests, bearing in mind Celtic's natural links with the Catholic community in Northern Ireland. However, to his credit Lennon continued to play for Northern Ireland, although it is by common consent that his performances were better for Celtic than Northern Ireland. Naturally this led to question marks over commitment and his club and religion reared their head in conversation.

This reached its zenith in the Norway game, when sections of the crowd booed Neil Lennon. I personally would never boo a player or a team I lend my support to, as it simply does no good to any interested parties. However, two schools of thought developed over the issue. First, the standard view was that Lennon was booed because of his poor performance in a dreadful team display. More damagingly though was the critical analysis that Lennon got the bird because he was Celtic playing Catholic and therefore had no place in a unionist bastion such as Windsor Park. Typically this opinion caught hold and the press had a field day, led on the mainland by the 'shock-tactics' Daily Mail, who sent a reporter to the next game (against the Czech Republic) and gave no coverage whatsoever to the game in a full page save the final paragraph. Obviously all the stories about sectarianism came out and what a dreadful place Windsor Park is, and the ground should be closed and the team be disbanded, thereby creating a united Ireland team like the rugby set-up.

However, I would like to like to say this incident was totally blown out of proportion and will explain why.

When Gavin first took me inside Windsor Park, I enjoyed the experience, but noted a banner by the corner flag on the apex of the North and Railway Stands suggesting 'NO CEASEFIRE AT WINDSOR PARK'. This was present at the Republic of Ireland game in November 1994, as were numerous so-called 'party songs', such the 'Sash', which in certain scenarios can be considered an inflammatory ditty and therefore not welcome in a football ground.

In a strange way, the banner, which was a direct reference to the then short-lived paramilitary 'ceasefire', made me feel somewhat ashamed and dirty, but I naturally kept my opinions to myself.

However, over the intervening seven years, these messages, banners and songs had largely disappeared as the IFA attempted to make Windsor Park a more inclusive arena, via community programmes and the like. I did not see that reported, even though I personally made representations to the Daily Mail, who took a totally unfair stance over this affair, which was wrong and deplorable, but little else. In conversation with other supporters, such an incident had never occurred before with Catholic players, even in the dark sectarian hate filled days of the 70s and 80s, and therefore there was little reason to occur then, save the players' performances, which appeared questionable to numerous elements.

Personally, I do not care who plays for Northern Ireland, as long as they fulfil the laid down credentials and win us the World Cup!

With the
future prime
minister of
Latvia
(Gerti)

Riga
1995

Yerevan
kitchen
crew

April
1997

There's
always
one!
Bangkok

May
1997

Green & White army awayday
Istanbul, Sept 1998

Ulstermen
with Manola
La Bomba

Santander
June 1998

Guess
Where?

Moldova
March
1999

Any questions?
Dortmund press centre

Sept 1999

The Slovak Czech
NI Supporters Club -
Hanke and Katarina

Taplice
June 2001

Three Amigos
John Aitkin and
Gavin Lavery

Vaduz
March 2002

Botanical
Gardens?
No Madrid
railway
station!

Madrid
Oct 2002

Public conveniences if you like?
Abovyan (Armenia), March 2003

Offensive weapon or what?
Abovyan, March 2003

Standing tall with Lenin
Donetsk, Sept 2003

Green & White Army social function

Donetsk Sept 2003

NI Supporters team – hung over and all.

Tallinn
March 2004

Curtly Ambrose & me

Antigua
May 2004

No! It's in Kingston,
Jamaica with
Yvonne Walsh

Jamaica
May 2004

Baku, Azerbaijan
October 2004

Travelling companion Robert Walsh - Rangers
Supporters Club

Baku, October 2004

Match day kit – 11 tone green!

Armenia 2003

David Beckham beware – with a left foot as well!
Supporters match

Donetsk
Sept 2004

EASTWARDS AGAIN

As mentioned, Northern Ireland's next fixture was a qualifying match against the Czech Republic and with the press hawks circling, the atmosphere was very withdrawn as Northern Ireland lost a close fought encounter 0-1. Though the team lost, it was at least a competitive performance and supporters seemed to draw solace from the team's fighting spirit, against one of European football's glamour teams.

However, John's attention and mine was turning to a trip to Bulgaria beginning the following Monday.

This trip had been shrouded in danger from the very start of planning, in early January, when the airline with whom we had booked, Balkans International Airlines, had its entire fleet grounded. The travel agent had managed to get Lufthansa to guarantee our tickets, but it did not stop them losing our baggage in their hub at Frankfurt. This was also where an hilarious 'Americanism' occurred.

When I was working at the Students' House groups of American students regularly came through the premises and it was always interesting to overhear what they said. They tended to follow like sheep and often asked 'What was good!' before buying a drink. I worked this out and tended to sell them something that was going out of date and was sweet: often incorporating cider and blackcurrant cordial. Also, they would talk about visiting the sights but suggesting, for example, Hyde Park Corner was where Germans were hung in World War II. I never interjected but had a great laugh at an American's expense when the flight attendant on the flight Sofia announced the destination and the man sitting by my window shouted, 'Ma'am I've got to get off, I'm going to Cairo!'.

I latterly told Gavin about this, to which he announced he had a fetish for taking the Mickey out of Americans, but wondered if this guy would have laughed about the luggage less Northern Ireland supporters.

Spring in Sofia, was the mildest for years with t-shirt weather the order and we really needed to change our socks and pants, which were 'crawling' by Tuesday night. Fortunately though, we had not gone on a skiing holiday like DJ Darren and his friends who I met up with at the Under-21 game in Vratsa. They also asked for help in getting hotel accommodation in Sofia, and this was where the lure of the silver dollar in the former Eastern Bloc kicked in.

Our hotel, the Niki, was a family run affair, with a few rooms above a bar/restaurant and was supposedly full, yet a phone call from a dollar paying client who had some friends at a loose end suddenly rendered rooms available at the $16 a night rate. This event was similar to my buying Marlboro cigarettes in the Chisnau market. At $6 for 200, a nice mark-up could be made in London on this commodity, but it was unwise to take the Russian blend with non-English writing on the packet. As the dollars were in the offing, the seller suddenly returned with the authentic American packeted Marlboro. Simply put, when you pay in dollars east of Prague, money (or branded labelled scotch) talks! This is because the economies are non-credit and you regularly see half built buildings which look like they have abandoned simply because the owner is short of money. Indeed in Armenia, in 2003 the hotel owner converted our dollars into sand and bricks within four hours of paying him.

At the Under-21 game, which we travelled to by train and home from via chartered taxis at the behest of Marty, at

$4 per head, I bumped into a quiet man who was in the official IFA party. This was Robert Walsh, a genial and pleasant person with whom I have travelled regularly since 2001, and who told me his stay with the IFA party was an expensive one; as his room mate had left the phone off the hook after ringing Belfast and left Robert with a $300 bill. Nothing such has (thankfully) happened since.

The Under-21 game was a forgetful affair, but typical of East European football had a fire engine and ambulance, which was donated courtesy of the North Staffordshire service on duty, parked at the edge of the cinder running track. This is always a trait of any football fixture in these parts of the world and probably a throwback to the communist era and a similar scenario ensued at the full fixture the day after.

It was almost a game John did not attend, because of his on-going 'sleeping sickness'. I always ask about John's health with a serious overtone, because he has great difficulty in sleeping at nights and is then tired during the day. His illness was acute in Sofia and combined with general sickness, he almost dodged out of the game and the walkabout in downtown Sofia on the morning of the match.

Wearing our colours, a man approached us in the street and asked if we were Marty. Giving a negative, he asked where he was, explaining that he was a member of the Belgrade Rangers Supporters' Club and had been in contact with Marty via the internet. Dangerous thing the internet, because Marty did not want to meet him, as he believed he was a hooligan looking for nothing more than a fight. I would not know whom he wanted to fight, as the local police looked 'angry' in complete riot gear and he was slightly outnumbered by the Bulgarian supporters!

There were some forty supporters in Sofia, with all the usual suspects in situ, along with a new group from

Bushmills, home of the same named whisky from the North Antrim coast. Ray and the boys have become regular fixtures on away trips and were present in Ukraine in 2003 and the Caribbean tour in 2004. Another loss was seen, as Northern Ireland went down 3-4; a somewhat flattering score line, as the score was 1-4, with two minutes remaining.

As is usual, the 'away' supporters were detained in the ground for a while and then received a full armoured escort as we were marched back to the Hotel Niki. This only seemed to bother those wishing to visit Kentucky Fried Chicken, but the marchers stopped for them.

Peculiarly in places like this, it does not seem to bother supporters when the team loses and I have deduced this is because most supporters are not going to let a losing team depress them when the drink is 25p a pint, vodka under £1 a bottle and the girls wear outrageously short skirts. The unofficial meeting point was a bar on a street corner by the Hilton and thereafter anywhere where the unofficial group leaders feel has an atmosphere. One such place was an unofficial strip joint, where we saw what will be an unnamed television journalist, leave as we were entering at 3 a.m! As can be deduced, the beer usually flows amongst supporters, often to numb the pain!

IN REVERSE

Northern Ireland did not use the late April friendly date; instead choosing to concentrate on the reverse spring fixtures with Bulgaria visiting Belfast and Northern Ireland playing their final match of the season in the Czech Republic. Bulgaria came to Belfast and produced a workman-like performance to win 0-1, but many eyes were looking towards the match in Teplice; around an hour North of Prague. It seemed everybody was going: the Portadown crowd, numerous of the Carrickfergus Band, Marty, and even Gavin Nixon.

I was travelling alone to this fixture, as I had some business to catch up on.

Katarina, from London was now studying back at home in Bratislava and I had contacted her and she was thrilled to offer me some hospitality. As such, I flew to Vienna, was met by her and a chauffeur friend, shipped into Slovakia and spent two days as a guest of her family.

This part of travel is important to me in that I can see how people actually live their lives and how it differs. I had been to Romania a few times over the past years to stay with friends I had met whilst travelling through Bucharest to Moldova and believe it or not, really enjoyed staying with a family in a grey high rise 'Stalinist' style apartment (top floor) and seeing how Romanians bought their food, dealt with queues at bus stops, and more worryingly how they dealt with the stray dogs which are literally everywhere. This is a throwback to the Caucaescu era, when he decided to systematise a peasant population by moving them into cities, complete with pets. Obviously the dog was the first thing to end up on the street, with orphans close behind.

For Katarina, life was better than this, as her father was involved in a fledgling market gardening business, and doing good business with an Italian distributor, whilst her mother was a teacher. Life was simple in a small village of some 5,000 called Gbely, and did not content Katarina, as she wanted the bright lights of the city. However, this was where her roots were and she took great pleasure in introducing her family, the youngest member of which, a seven-year old sister, spent days before my arrival saying 'Hello Shaun. Welcome to Slovakia and our family.' It was a really nice thought and I was not sure if this small village had ever seen an English tourist before, as the whole of Katarina's mother's school seemed to stop when we paid a brief visit one morning. I put it down to the green trainers!

We then met Katarina's grandfather; a proud man who impressed me greatly with his self-sufficiency. His garden was full of fruit and vegetables, including the most divine sweet cherries, and sheds full of rabbits, breeding for food, along with all kinds of mechanical motors and tools. Katarina explained her grandfather, who spoke no English, but was a Liverpool supporter, grew vegetables and bred rabbit to feed his family while his country was occupied first by Nazis and then the communists, and food was strictly rationed. He also made motors to provide some light during years of power cuts.

So proud and so pleasant a man as you could ever wish to meet, I was saddened in 2004 when Katarina said age was beginning to catch up with him and he had stopped breeding rabbits. You do not see this from the four walls of a hotel room.

The day before the game, we transferred from Gbely, via Prague: a city rapidly changing from the dour sight I recalled on a brief visit to watch England in 1992, to Usti nad Labem, in the North of the Czech Republic. This was around 20 kilometres from Teplice, and the home to Hana, one of Katarina's friends whom she had met in

London. She was going to put us up for a couple of nights, and was going to attend the game with Katarina and me.

Hana (or Hanky as I call her), in my opinion is everything Katarina aspires to be. Highly intelligent, organised, and aware of the world in which she lives, with the luck you make and the pitfalls it brings.

They both came to nanny in England to improve their English, but whilst Katarina was young and free, England was more of a career break for Hanky, as she had a boyfriend in Usti and a stable lifestyle, and could get work anytime in a secretarial or language skills field. Indeed in 2004 she was employed both as a married mother, to husband Franki, and daughter Anna, and as a translator, working on legal documents for the President of Lindt chocolate, earning a cool $4,000 a month: a king's ransom in that part of the world.

However, when I visited, she became a member, for one day of the rapidly growing 'Green and White Army'. One figure put the support at 700 for this game; most of whom, of course, stayed in Prague. What could be better than cheap booze, cheap food, sexy women and football for an occasional 'away' supporter: and not forgetting the sites of Wenceslas Square and Charles Bridge. Robert Walsh and his wife, Yvonne, were caught on the Astronomical Clock/Cathedral Square tourist trail as me and Katrina briefly passed through on our train journey.

Katarina had her own shirt and scarf, which I gave her whilst in London, and I loaned Hanky another green strip, which they complimented with green hair bands, lipstick, nail varnish and of course face paint and hair dye. Afterwards, both unilaterally said it was the best day out they had ever had, as the Northern Ireland supporters managed to out cheer the Czechs, particularly in the second half, with an 'up-down' rendition of 'Sammy McIlroy's Green and White Army'. This is where one group of supporters, often in the lower part of the stand will give the aforementioned chant, followed by a rest, as the upper deck take over, and so on. Psychological maybe, but I am sure the team performed better with this support, and held the Czechs to 1-1, before the last five minutes, when the home team bagged two late goals.

Hanky and Katarina's days were made as we headed back to the railway station, when they gave their thoughts to Czech national television, suggesting they were glad the Czechs had won, but had had such an enjoyable, adrenalin filled day as guests of the Northern Ireland supporters; most of whom had gone back to Prague by coach. Indeed I feel Northern Ireland's 'away' support was truly born that day, as it was organised, with coaches, meeting points in bars in Prague and the like, rather than just being ad-hoc. (Numerous asked 'When's the next one (trip)?') It was a pity nobody told the police authorities though, as at a loose estimate, there were two hundred police, of various guises from riot to horseback, waiting to shepherd what were ultimately two female and one male supporter back to Prague (or rather Usti). Nonetheless, I would no longer be 'singing on my own'.

Katarina is a perpetual student struggling (as ever) to make ends meet in Munster (Germany) and working in a bakery, but I have the utmost respective for her, in that she is young and enjoys her free spirit, which was denied her in her formative years thanks to political ideology. Hanky on the other hand is a diary-keeping professional mum, creating great personal wealth thanks to her education and has an impressive lifestyle, so much so I have visited her three times since the Northern Ireland game. One occasion was courtesy of a free flight from Go (now part of Easyjet) in October 2001, when Hanky became the first and only member of the 1st Slovak/Czech Northern Ireland Supporters Club, thanks to a fleece jacket produced by Jim Rainey. She wears it well!

MAJBRITT (OOPS!)

Travel to Denmark in early September for the Northern Ireland fixture, was a first for me as I never visited before, but even after this brief sorte, which lasted less than 24 hours, I was in love with the place. So much so, that I cannot understand why people do not emigrate in numbers to this place. Even in the Copenhagen city centre, people just leave their flats with a lock of their door, rather than gating, bolting and hoping. For me, I would gladly forego cheap booze and tobacco for that relative safety Denmark brings, and I deduced this is why few Brits emigrate to, or even holiday in, Denmark. I am convinced Britain is broadly a nation of alcoholics and often emigrate for sunshine, yes, but often because lager is cheap.

It is certainly not in Denmark, with a beer often more than £4, but no town centre drink fuelled violence on Saturday nights. Furthermore, I think a health service, where you get a consultation immediately or a year's full paid maternity leave is worth paying into, even if income tax is 60%.

I arrived at 2 p.m. on the day of the game to be met by Gavin and John who had been over for a few days, and after a quick hotel check-in, decided to show off my new departure for away games: fancy dress, incorporating wig, face paint, trainers, green strip and ultimately whatever else I can find applicably green. This has developed with hats, cloaks, boots, leg warmers, trousers and a coat. Indeed, my girlfriend Rebecca gets, what she terms as 'grouchy' when I check in all kinds of shops to on weekend breaks to see if there is any suitable green kit around.

Copenhagen's locals seemed to enjoy the 'green way', as we headed to the famous wharf on all the postcards for a few drinks.

Places like this are fun pre-match, as supporters from both sides meet ,chant, shout, hollow and drink. There is no trouble when and amongst Northern Ireland supporters, unlike England fans, when riot police are controlling bar areas. As mentioned earlier, this scenario is important to me, and continued on the journey to the functional Parkenstadion. Some 180 supporters made the trip, to witness a fighting 1-1 draw from the most obstructive viewing corner in the stadium. The performance was typical of Northern Ireland in that it was 'backs to the wall' defensive spirit that delivered the goods and started a pleasant night's celebrations.

We headed to the town centre bars near Tivoli Gardens and ended up in a Scottish bar, which initially had a somewhat deflated atmosphere, as news and highlights were fed through the television of England's amazing 1-5 win against the Germans in Munich. People were coming and going on their Saturday night out, but a lady came by to see what was happening and ended up chatting to us. Majbritt was very amiable and in a nutshell, we spent the rest of the night together, with her taking me to the airport the following morning. Sure this sort of thing had happened before (Munich 1996), but this time it was (hopefully) different and she invited me back to Denmark, which was when I learned about the lifestyle Danes tend to lead. A third visit in November left us going our separate ways, as distance again just got in the way. I did find myself falling in love with Majbritt, but was deluding myself that long distance (phone) relationships could work. Majbritt wanted someone to go to the cinema with, or cuddle up close to whilst watching television. As I was living in France, of course I was not that person. The person and the place did have an effect though, as I try to holiday in different parts of Denmark at least once a year. I enjoy the tranquility and the friendliness and honesty of the Danes, not to mention their fierce national pride, with most houses flying a Danish flag outside the house, with new houses often having a flag pole as standard. I was even on the point of moving there in spring of 2002 following my departure from French, but the job I had lined fell through as the company involved filed for insolvency in the USA.

Of course the issues in Denmark were on my mind, the following Wednesday when Northern Ireland took on Iceland, seeking revenge for the embarrassment last October. It came in an impressive 3-0 victory and I consider it the last time Northern Ireland played well between then and a 3-0 win against Trinidad and Tobago at the end of the Caribbean tour in June 2004.

However, before departing on the public transport hike to Belfast, I had an inkling something was in the offing at work. Owners Neil and Marco had been in France a lot around late August, which was unusual as they operated a very laissez-faire style, leaving the shops to get on with it as far as possible, whilst they played with their 'classic' Ferraris or flew around the world watching cricket or rugby.

My worst fears came true, when I returned from a visit to see Majbritt in late September. Neil came to see me, and suggested the shop was to close early the following month. Fortunately in France, you cannot just be made redundant if this occurs, and I was to move to be Jean-Michel's deputy at the large shop on the industrial estate close to the motorway. I looked on this as a very short-term measure for, as explained, manager Jean-Michel was impossible to work for. To be fair though, Neil saw me 'right' financially with a nice pay-off, which was to be paid by Majestic Wine, whom he sold the business to some three weeks later, for a cool £7million in cash. This explained his need to close what I term 'my shop', and the financial sweetener.

The actual closure date was early October, which coincided with a Northern Ireland trip to Malta for the last group match.

This time I booked a flight and hotel separately and certainly was not on a pensioners spring break, like some eighteen months before. I took an Air Malta night flight and made sure I stayed in the more atmospheric St.Julians, inclusive of Gareth Cornett, who was so drunk post game that he saw fit to direct the traffic around the winding streets, avoiding those drinking (and sleeping) in the gutter and the mini-skirted tourists looking for a party venue.

As for the game, the only thing at stake was pride and Northern Ireland delivered the goods courtesy of a David Healy penalty against a Malta side which provided great nuisance value. Nowadays the phrase is that weak teams 'park the bus (in front of the goals)', an analogy for packing the defence and hoping the opposing team do not score and end up frustrating a goalless draw. Then the weak team suggest they are improving by getting (frustrating) results.

Whilst forgetful as a spectacle, the game did throw up an odd incident in that both Sammy McIlroy and his deputy Jim Harvey were sent from the dug out by the referee. This occurs when the match officials have reason that team managers and the like have broken the (admin) rules and on this occasion it led to David Currie being in charge of team affairs from the dug out whilst incommunicado, via mobile phone, with Messrs McIlroy and Harvey.

If this and the home victory are excluded, as every other team beat Malta home and away, the team record in the group showed just one win and two draws from the matches. Hardly satisfactory, but , as mentioned over the period of this group a 'family' of supporters had developed, managing to get to most games. Numerous have been mentioned, like Robert, (Gareth) Corney and Marty, who got to every game, but others like John, Darren and Sam, who cherry picked games were also most welcome and a hard core of support was pleasant to see at every game. This was, and has been supplanted by Jim Rainey and Alan Ferris, who have developed the support via the 'amalgamation' of Northern Ireland Supporters Clubs. Indeed, in simple conversation, Stephen Beacom, chief football scribe of the Belfast Telegraph has termed the support a 'cult', which is growing as people dip in and out of Northern Ireland's foreign support, enjoy what is seen and done and get 'hitched'. However, one trait I have noticed amongst these fellow travellers is that the match result is not so very important. Sure it's great to see the team you support win, but this does not happen so often with Northern Ireland and as such, any win is a serious bonus. 'Winning' also occurs for the local bar owners and shopkeepers who seem to do particularly well when Northern Ireland are in town. The bar outside the team hotel in Donetsk (Ukraine) ran out of beer and in Zurich in 2004, wine sales seemed to take a steep upward scale for three days, as a bottle of local plonk, matched the price for two cans. However, on a positive note, I have never seen this family the worse for wear and causing a public disturbance. Drunk yes, falling asleep inside grounds due to the drink yes, and sick and hungover the morning after, yes, but trouble causing in foreign cities, certainly not. Indeed the inclusivity of some home town supporters is also a very welcoming experience, as often they will be happy to buy you a drink and know your business, particularly in English speaking Scandinavia. Surely this is what following an international team is about, rather than being hoarded on and off and in and out of planes, buses and grounds by riot police.

THE MED – AGAIN!

The winter of 2001/02 was tempered by the arranging of a Northern Ireland friendly in February in Cyprus against Poland, leading therefore to a return to the Mediterranean at a very accommodating time of year. Personally, I find hot sunshine and a fortnight lying on a beach in high summer a complete non-starter, because being fair-skinned I burn easily and also do not like to feel hot, thirsty and sweaty. However, a warm Cyprus in February, escaping the chill of Northern France, was most appealing.

It is also appealing to many club and national teams for the same reasons, in that teams can get together in warm weather, set up training camps and work on team bonding, if nothing else. Apparently there were some 30 teams in situ, from African national junior squads to Hungarian club team Ferencvros, whilst I visited the island and the local press quoted this situation as a booming avenue for tourism. There is always an invitational international tournament at the time of year, but Northern Ireland were not involved, though they were to play on the same pitch after the 3rd/4th play off of said tournament.

Watching that game, between Switzerland and Hungary was a most surreal experience. Robert, who I had hooked up with in Larnaca, and me actually stood on the touchline by the advertising hoardings and chatted to the assistant referee throughout this, a full international. World Soccer latterly quoted the attendance as 100 for this match, which was a most generous figure, and physically swelled by groups of Northern Ireland supporters who duly arrived for the main event. For the

Northern Ireland game the supporters, were shepherded in the nicest possible way into a granstand.

Northern Ireland supporters present at this event, witnessed an incident after 18 minutes which, though insignificant at the time gradually became more and more important and WILL play a part in these memoirs. Steven Lomas' header into the Poles net started an exact two-year goal drought for Northern Ireland, only broken by David Healy in Belfast in February 2004. For the record, Northern Ireland were a distant second in this game, losing 1-4, to a Polish side who were fancied as a dark-horse in the forthcoming World Cup Finals in the Far East.

On a personal level, the game was played in Limassol, which meant transferring from my base in Larnaca. Buses ran regularly, but not after tea-time, which meant a car had to be hired, in conjunction with Robert. I asked the hotel receptionist about this and she pointed me to an office literally across the street. Her pointing came via a fur-coated arm and she was sitting in front of an electric fire.

Now imagine the situation. It is mid-February, and I have arrived, via a skiing holiday in Romania, where I spent 90% of my time on my arse, in mid-60s degree Cyprus. The wind is warm and the air temperature ambient so naturally I have donned my shorts and match strip and felt the need to get some pleasant and welcome spring sunshine on my body. Yet one native is in fur and hugging a fire. She quite literally questioned my intelligence and thought I must be mad. I explained the weather was like summer in the UK, and I had been in the Piona Brasov ski resort the previous weekend with temperatures freezing at best. The lady wished me well as I took the directions to cross the street, but I was convinced she thought I was an extra-terrestrial.

More 'fun' was in hand at the car-hire office, as I was joined by Robert. The owner was happy to loan a car with a 100 mile distance limit for a price of 15 Cypriot pounds (£Cy): around £18. However, he demanded an £Cy30 deposit. Asking why, the owner, who doubled as a Warner Brothers criminal, complete with cigarette in the side of the mouth, explained that the British were the worse at getting out of bed in the summer to get flights home. He was sick of loaning the offenders cars and then going to the airport to collect them because it was the only way late Brits could get to the airport.

The ensuing hired Daewoo, was a wreck to put it mildly, but it got us to and from doing a maximum of 50 mph uphill (downhill was better), returning with a very drunken Robert at midnight. He had been taxied all day and was the worse for wear, whilst I was totally sober, but looking forward to a few drinks after returning. Not alone though, but this was how it turned out as Robert fell asleep in the hotel bar; drink in hand.

RETURN TO LIECHTENSTEIN

Northern Ireland's March fixture was a friendly away trip to Liechtenstein: a match I was very much looking forward to. I had been to Vaduz in October 1995 and wanted to see if this overtly sleepy, playground of the rich had changed.

The lady was still stamping passports for 5 Swiss Francs in the post office and you could still buy your cow-bell trinkets, jumbo sized pencils and stamp selections from the tourist shops. However, as I mentioned earlier, a dual carriageway approaching the town, complete with McDonald's drive-thru and furniture showrooms, was now in situ and it seemed to wreck the post card image.

Having stayed and been bored in Zurich twice over the years, I decided to stay in a similar post card style town in Sargans, just outside the Liechtenstein border, but commutable by the yellow post-bus. The said buses, connect the small towns and villages in the area, including Vaduz, Buchs and Sargans and run perfectly on time, literally carrying bags of post to and fro as required. It seems almost historical in action, but is peculiarly pleasant.

Sargans was a typical small affluent continental town, with a row of designer clothes shops, numerous taverns and small supermarket. It was proudly postering itself as the home town of Swiss world number one tennis star Martina Hingis and had a small schloss (castle) which overlooked the town. On meeting Gavin and John at the railway station, I decided we would have a look at said castle, for no other reason than it may offer a photographic view and kill some time.

The place doubled as both castle and restaurant and we were fortunate in being allowed to dine in these most opulent surroundings as long as we had the salad menu. It was too good an opportunity to miss, dining at a round table sitting by knight's armour, swords, flintlocks and other weapons of mass destruction from the middle ages. The hostess even allowed us into a museum type area where we had the opportunity to actually play with the swords etc. should we have liked. On leaving, I could well imagine the affluent Swiss having a black-tie dinner party drinking fine wine (I saw the wine cellar) and dining on the most expensive items, and then saying they dined in a castle as a matter of course. The experience was certainly better than sitting outside a bar all afternoon and it is these little privileges, similar to our wandering around the Westphalen stadium and sitting in the press conference seats, that can make airport departure halls and delayed trains worthwhile.

Football wise, Liechtenstein were getting their house in order, with FC Vaduz challenging to join the top flight of the Swiss league, and the country having a new and very functional national stadium, with a capacity of some 3,500. It is often a talking point as to why Northern Ireland do not have a stadium and the word 'cost' comes to the fore, but surely a similar stadium, multi-purpose if necessary, could be built for a snip of the £700million it is costing to build a new Wembley.

Liechtenstein was in England's qualifying group and were probably looking for UK style opposition in this friendly, and they found a combative spirit in Northern Ireland, but little else. In a nutshell, the performance witnessed by the 27 supporters was dreadful, but in my opinion not as poor as the 1997 nemesis against Albania. I was in a minority of one, but no-one else went to that game, as supporters led by Marty began to 'boo' the team.

I do not object to this behaviour because I work on the premise that if you have paid to be entertained and you consider it unsatisfactory, then you have a right to be aggrieved and make your views known. However, I keep my feelings to myself because 'booing' is unsupportive and does nothing to help anyone. An international team does not play bad on purpose and if things do not work out, then the management will surely know and, as such unilateral booing serves no purpose. I did think about it though and put the thought down to being bored with both the match and taking the 'Mickey' out of a stereotypical red-cheeked, bearded and bellied ex-pat Irish man, who had turned up to watch the wrong Ireland and was a Manchester United supporter! As I said to Marty, these types are fair game for a little (fun) banter and he considers them like Marmite: you either love them or hate them, but I am sure he was smiling after seeing our performance.

The game in Liechtenstein was slightly overshadowed by the draw and ensuing fixture dates for the Euro 2004 qualifying series starting in September. The draw had thrown up top seeds Spain, Ukraine, Greece, and Armenia in the group but a log-jam had occurred since January over the group fixture dates because the respective associations could not agree who was travelling where and when. In such circumstances arbitration ensues via a randomly computer generated fixture list and was of a concern to President Jim Boyce, who also suggested in conversation that Kazahkstan wanted Northern Ireland to be the first country in UEFA to play them.

Kazahkstan had been allowed to join the UEFA club, by successfully arguing such an opportunity would enhance their standard of football. Not surprisingly, few associations wanted to play them, given the fact to travel would mean something like a ten hour flight to capital Alamaty from Western Europe. Perhaps the Kazahk president wanted to bring East and West UEFA together, with Northern Ireland obviously a far-away outpost from their respective view! The fixture has yet to come to pass, but by the team supporters reached Zurich airport for the flight home, UEFA had made the long awaited fixture draw.

News filtered through that Northern Ireland were to sit out the September fixture, beginning their campaign in October with a trip to Spain followed by home fixture against Ukraine. Interspersed with chit-chat about said fixtures and holidays was Marty suggesting his workmates at the RAF had clubbed together to create a rather morbid sweep.

It incorporated punters paying in to bet on the next famous person to pass away. Of course, luminaries such as the Pope, Robert Mugabe, Bin Laden, Maggie Thatcher and the then living Queen Mother were mentioned. Slightly the worse for Erdinger Hefeweiss wheat beer, I mentioned, much to the amusement of a career woman standing behind me, that I felt the Queen Mother lived in ice suspension to keep her alive, and was thawed out for her public appearances, circling around Royal Ascot, the Highland Games and Christmas at Sandringham. I was latterly somewhat embarassed, when the following Saturday, a news flash during Grandstand announced the death of the Queen's mother.

I mentioned to the queue that I was happy with the draw, as I could review Armenia and Ukraine six years on, visit Greece for the first time, and return to Spain to see Margarita Cobo.

Margarita was a typically beautiful Spanish lady, with imposing dark eyes and matching hair, who came to ask me for bar work at International Students' House, as her best Spanish friend Angela had told her the scenario would improve her English. She was at college in London learning both English and how to have a good time, and whilst terming her eccentric is unfair, she was certainly different.

Her natural beauty meant she always had to work hard as males always demanded to be served by her and she could not understand why at a show at the Royal Albert Hall, she felt everyone was looking at her, dressed in a leather micro skirt and knee length boots! Furthermore, she once asked me 'What a COW was?', because a family she latterly lived with had internal strife and the husband was permanently terming his wife such an animal. Margarita thought it was something else!

I had visited Margarita for her birthday in 1998 and with (French) David and his girlfriend Tracey in 2001 and on both occasions had a great time; complete with tickets for a Madrid derby and a Champions League match featuring Real Madrid and Lazio. Whether Northern Ireland would play in Madrid was doubtful, but I was going to visit Margarita regardless.

GROUP WARM UP

Coincidentally, Northern Ireland had arranged for Spain to visit Belfast for the April friendly, which doubled as a 20-year celebration of Northern Ireland's finest footballing hour, when they beat the 1982 World Cup hosts in Valencia.

The supporters club's held a dinner at Belfast's opulent Culloden Hotel, which I could not attend, but Roy Bennett of the 3rd Carrickfergus Silver Band arranged a different kind of entertainment.

Roy and his partner Denise had been involved in the trip to Lisbon in 1997 and we had been on good terms since, occasionally getting together for a game of golf prior to home games. However, spring 2002 had seen floods and more floods, rendering the golf course unplayable and instead Roy had pulled a couple of strings to get himself, Dessie, Gavin (Lavery) and me into Belfast Town Hall for a pre-match junket.

Belfast Town Hall is a most imposing structure which dominates the centre of Belfast, creating an island of grass (for summer picnics) and administration around which local buses and shoppers commute. The structure inside is similarly as one would expect with miles of dark panelled corridors supporting impressions of Ulsters's civic heroes. It also supported a rather personal mayoral hospitality suite which we used with the Lord Mayor of Belfast for at least an hour, signing the guest book, which included the autographs of Bill Clinton and Prince Edward.

On departure, I was brought back down to earth as I fought to enter a mobbed Hunter's Bar, which is the unofficial pre-match meeting point, to meet Lesley from the Irish F.A.

Lesley's job, in my opinion, is a thankless one, as she is mainly the I.F.A.'s tele-receptionist, which means answering the phone all day long and passing those on the line to respective extensions. It is something which I could never have the patience to do, but I had got to know Lesley via this, and her occupation. Indeed, our first major telephone discussion occurred a couple of years earlier, when French post service, La Poste, lost a packet containing four tickets for the Champions League Final, taking place in Paris.

The game, which climaxes the European club football season, took place, as usual, on a Wednesday night in late May, with Lesley posting the tickets from the IFA the preceding Thursday. They landed in France at 1215p.m. on the Saturday, yet it took another five days for them to reach Calais; arriving on the Thursday after the Valencia v Real Madrid extravaganza. Lesley, David Currie, La Poste and ourselves, as David did the talking, lobbied UEFA and the ticket printer at Stade du France, to successfully print some duplicates, but five days to get a 'special post' packet 60 miles across Northern France is a little worrying!

It was impossible to get a drink in Hunter's that night, as poignancy and a classy opposition had sold out Windsor Park, causing major pub traffic so I dragged Lesley and boyfriend Paul outside, in search of a drink. We could not even get into an off-licence or the emergency snooker club bar on the Lisburn Road, and we ended up inside the ground 45 minutes prior to kick-off, with a grouchy Paul munching on a hamburger: commonly known as Windsor 'carpet-burgers', given their questionable standard.

Paul makes a day of Northern Ireland games, taking an afternoon off work, enjoying a few drinks with his old school-buddies like Darren and Michael, meeting Lesley and me, having a flutter in the bookies, and then being 'entertained' by Northern Ireland. A drink prior to kick-off can be a duel edged sword in that you may need to wee prior to half time, or the alcohol can numb the pain of spectating. However, no alcohol can make the affair more serious, hence Paul's state of mind.

I now sit next to Paul and Lesley for the first half of Belfast games and then move up the stairs to join Harry Simpson's group booking for the second half, as I feel obliged because that is where my seat and my other acquaintances sit. Also there is the chance of winning the hat sweep, entry £1, winner takes all, value around £15.

I have never 'won', but Spain certainly won that evening netting five times, giving a footballing masterclass, courtesy of world class players such as Raul, Morientes and Baraja. Worryingly, we had to play Spain for real over the next eighteen months, and many were wondering what would actually happen.

EASY SUMMER

Northern Ireland chose not to play any more friendlies prior to the summer World Cup Finals, instead looking forward to a pre-qualifying Euro 2004 friendly with Cyprus in August.

Personally, I had a great summer recess, because on return to Calais in early May, I was informed there was no worthwhile job in the wine warehouse any more and I was offered a huge pay-off. I did not need a second chance and quickly left France, though not where I anticipated.

I had lined up a marketing job in Denmark, but the charity that I was to work for had financial problems and instead I ended up staying with Keith and Sarah Pollitt and new baby Freya in their pub in North Wales for the summer.

Keith and Sarah are tenants of an idyllic country pub in Halkyn, North Wales, which overlooks the Dee and Mersey estuaries. I have had a great relationship with them and their three boxer dogs over the years, often getting Keith a barrel of beer for personal consumption over Christmas.

They put me up over the summer, because I was in work limbo, unable to take up employment immediately, as I had arranged to take my father to South Africa in early August to see his sister, for his 65th birthday present. As such, it would be unreasonable to expect a prospective employer to honour a week's holiday within a month of starting work and therefore I decided to take a summer off lounging around, watching cricket and doing some casual work.

The South Africa experience became a worry as it approached because my Dad had never been on a plane further than the Isle of Man from Blackpool and he was about to go long haul to South Africa, via a change over in Paris. Apart from his sickness on the first day, due no doubt to nerves, I needn't have worried, because he and Auntie Barbara never stopped talking and partying from arrival to departure.

I withdrew and listened intently to some of the hilarious chat, including tales of my father's estranged step-mother taking bags of charity shop clothes as a present to South Africa, and my dad and aunt stealing deposit paying pop bottles from the post office in Moorland Road near their childhood home.

I was a little sad on departure, because Barbara's husband (David) said the visit had made his wife ten years younger and I am sure I actually saw my Dad shed a tear. He was, and is a strong man, who grew up without a mother in austere post-war years, working seven days a week, excepting Christmas and Boxing Days, and hence could probably never shed a tear in case it was seen as humiliating. If a tear did appear, then that visit must have meant a lot and I am glad we took the trouble.

I also took the trouble shortly after my return to travel to Luton to look at taking on a new job as manager of the university student union. I was offered the post and took the job the weekend before Northern Ireland played the Cyprus fixture.

Cyprus are a weak team and probably chosen the way Germany choose the likes of Liechtenstein pre-World Cup, for winning moral boosting fodder. However, if the script is not read, things can backfire.

Also, if the media is to be believed, clubs do not want their players released for such fixtures, as it is early season, players may not be fully fit, and clubs may need their employees on board as playing styles develop. Therefore international squads are regularly bereft of players with suspicious strains and pulls.

The flip side of this is the chance for international managers to study fringe players or bleed youngsters from the Under-21 squad. Hence on this occasion, Sammy McIlroy brought youngsters Michael Ingham, Michael Duff, Warren Feeney and Stephen Robinson into the squad, but he was not ready for the incidents that occurred at tea-time, some three hours before kick-off.

The Belfast (Evening) Telegraph carried a story that Neil Lennon's family had received a death threat, threatening safety if Lennon took the pitch against Cyprus. Tempers had already been frayed over this Lennon issue in the lead up to the game, as a graffitted sign suggesting 'Lennon RIP' had appeared on a wall in Lennon's home town of Lurgan.

Quite rightly, Lennon pulled out, never to be seen in Northern Ireland shirt again, but the ramifications were serious. Simply, by making a threat, an idiot could help select a Northern Ireland team, which is simply unacceptable in anyone's language. Unfortunately, Northern Ireland have such a small pool of players that they cannot and never have been able to lose a player of Lennon's stature, regardless of his club and religion, through anything unnatural. Lennon played for one of the biggest clubs in Europe and even if he did not perform in his combative way on the pitch for Northern Ireland as many anticipated, he should still have been allowed to add his experience to the squad whether as a player or squad member. This was taken away and must have put McIlroy's plans into disarray for what became a very subdued match and was unsurprisingly a 0-0 draw.

As a final thought, I would have 'retired' from international football in similar circumstances, because simply why would someone on a supposed £30,000 a week and secure employer to boot want any hassle of this nature.

SPAIN VIA ESBJERG

Though available, Northern Ireland did not take a fixture in early September, instead looking towards to the autumn games against Spain and Ukraine.

The trip to Spain commenced in the unlikely place of Esbjerg, a small port town on the west coast of Denmark: the airport which acts mainly as a transfer to and from oil-rigs. However, Ryanair fly there and this was important as I had booked to fly to Spain from Copenhagen. This was because I had made bookings in early summer on the proviso that I was going to work in Denmark. Therefore to save losing the flights I booked to travel to Esbjerg and then transfer via train to Copenhagen.

I consider the west coast of Denmark one of the most peaceful and idyllic places in the world with forests mixing with beaches in a strange kind of ruggedness which compliments the strong clean air.

Obviously, I had little time to enjoy the town, heading off to Madrid the day after via the capital and a stop-off in Brussels.

Thankfully, Margarita was at the airport and she directed me to the rail ticket office immediately post hug and kisses. She said the train to Albacete, where the game was being played, and would be a perfect Ryanair destination, as it is in the middle of nowhere, was an Inter-City destination and operated a strictly reserved seating policy. It was a good job she did, as the train was full and numerous supporters were left behind as the train departed.

Margarita had also booked me a hotel and, with her lover Peter, took me out for a most enjoyable evening tinged with a little jealousy. Dressed in typically elegant clothes, Margarita looked beautiful and I would have loved to have got 'closer', as I had wanted to in London on many occasions. However, I never did as she was a work colleague who became a friend and a moment of weakness would have ruined this. Also in catering, there is an old saying, 'that you do not screw the hourly paid!', as return favours can often be blackmailed. On this occasion Peter might not have been very accommodating, should I have made a pass!

As mentioned, Albacete is a large town miles away from anywhere with little hotel accommodation, (rendering me to sleep on Corney's bedroom floor) and a small ground holding only around 17,000.

Apparently the game was played here because it was the new Spanish manager's home town and consistent with Spain's policy of taking internationals around the country, save for Northern Basque and Catalonian lands, where there is a groundswell for state independence.

The game was played at the ridiculously late time of 9.45 pm. This is a policy which has been developed in Spain, with teams such as Real Madrid and Barcelona often playing at midnight for television ratings purposes. A great idea also for the drinkers in tow, but imagine a 9.45p.m. kick-off in England with supporters in the pub all day, but after the game one could conclude that Spain could have played Northern Ireland at 9.45 in the morning! They strolled to a 3-0 win, leaving the 700+ supporters disappointed but hardly surprised.

Many of those 700 were staying in Alicante, taking advantage of easy flying routes to and from the UK. Among those were the team and Malcolm Brodie, who stayed in the same hotel (and rumour has it room) as he did when Northern Ireland beat Spain twenty years previously. Of course, lightning did not strike twice, and it never did throughout the whole of the qualifying campaign, for as mentioned, Northern Ireland did not score throughout the eight games. However, on the bright side (if there is such a thing in all this) it must be noted that throughout the next seven games Northern Ireland only conceded five more goals.

This was because Northern Ireland were generally sound at the back with players playing regular club and Premiership football, including Maik Taylor (keeper) and Aaron Hughes (defence). Further up front though the strikers were permanently struggling for matches with Healy rarely starting for Preston and James Quinn often injured, although he became rejuvenated when he transferred to the Willem II outfit in Holland.

Monday saw the trek home via a ride in Margarita's car, which was a story in itself, because she had bought it off a friend who had won it in a supermarket raffle. I am always very sceptical of such things, as it usually incorporates getting a scratch card from a cashier, and putting name address and phone number on the back as you unsurprisingly have a winning card along with everyone else. The supermarket then creates a cheap database with said addresses, sending all kinds of crap in the post and gives a car and a few holidays away. Margarita's friend came home one day with a bright yellow Megane, leaving me with the thought that 'if you ain't in you ain't gonna win!', and me buying a lottery ticket for the next few Saturdays!

A night home in Luton was followed by a rare two night trip to Belfast for the Ukraine game. Surprisingly I was looking forward to this trip because I could touch base with a few friends, rather than merely country hopping to and from a game. I had got into the habit, because of travelling time to and from France, of visiting the province just for the games and little else. It took upwards of nine hours to get from Belfast to Calais if all the connections worked, which is a days' travel or a days' holiday. This time though I could relax and enjoy!

Enjoy I did, as I got a rare glimpse of the Under-21s at home and an even rarer glimpse of the inside of a salt mine.

Roy's partner Denise is the admin manager of the Carrickfergus Salt Company, which mines half a million tonnes of salt a year from two miles under the agricultural land away from the coast. She arranged for me, Roy and Tim Glover to have a show around on the afternoon before the game. This is a great rarity, as guests, save for occasional PhD students, are a no-no. The salt mine was absolutely dry underground which surprised me, as we were taken to see unblasted seams and the salt being shaken to make the crystals small enough to spread on the roads (mostly in the USA) over the winter. David, our host, made some great explanatory facts including the story that no salt from the Carrickfergus mine is spread in Northern Ireland, because the company only operates on economies of scale, filling cargo boats to the east coast of America.

It is occurrences like this that I really enjoy in Northern Ireland now, as I mentioned the football is usually a quick visiting experience. As such, I visit for non-footballing experiences, which usually include visiting bars, restaurants and houses with the 3rd Carrickfergus Silver Band. Simply, I enjoy the company of the likes of Dessie, whose house we usually end up for late night parties, and Tim whose demeanour is strangely infectious. He found out that Keith and I had decided to get some geese from a farm to keep the grass down and this had rancoured with Sarah who felt threatened by such beasts. She went to the local hairdresser and he asked her how things were at the pub and she replied that I was staying and it was good company. Adding to that, she then said that she was concerned about a few things, most obviously that Keith and I had been out to get a bag of cement off a neighbour and come home with three geese! This story just makes Tim, a sixteen stone gentle giant, crease with laughter.

As for the football, it appeared the Ukrainians came to Belfast determined not to lose, and with Northern Ireland unable to score, a 0-0 draw was inevitable: not a bad result in the circumstances and at least it put a point on the board having played the top two teams.

WINTER NIGHTMARE

As usual, the team went into winter hibernation, resurfacing in February for a friendly at home to Finland. Personally, though I was enduring a nightmare with work.

A couple of years on, I can say University of Luton Students' Union was without doubt the worst place I have ever worked.

I consider myself honest at all times when dealing with other people's money and did not differentiate whilst at Luton. However, it appeared most others had arranged some sort of 'Spanish' working practices helping to feather their nests. I tried to stop this, as the business finances were collapsing, and got rather nasty responses as a consequence, including being threatened in the street, staff arranging boycotts and generally destroying team morale from management down to casual staff. I stuck at it, whilst others were quite openly plotting and senior management did not want to get involved. It was a lonely existence and not easy not being able to explain what was occurring and I felt I needed some personal comfort away from Luton.

If I had been financially stable, I would have walked out of this job before Christmas, such was the now mutual contempt, and stacked shelves somewhere, but this was a non-starter as expensive excursions to Armenia and Ukraine were in the offing. Instead I decided to play the dating game, visiting pubs and clubs and even playing on the internet, looking for diversionary friendship and maybe even a shoulder to cry on.

I have watched the dating game from the safety of a bar servery and find people most interesting as people pose, study, approach, and get a response. Men are fun to watch as they often attack in packs, get on the dance floor, get knocked back from the mini-skirted crowd and come back to the bar and get paralytic on tequila shots. Girls are different as they as they seem more studious, can refuse and seem to enjoy destroying a man's ego, whilst visiting the toilet in umbilical pairs. Now I was playing.

I felt uncomfortable in Luton and went to the more up-market Harpenden; one train stop away. It was OK but I felt like I was in a common meat market and though some dates were fun with nice people, something was missing. I went on one date in Swansea with a woman who had a disturbed daughter who decided she had broke her leg in the shopping centre which almost put me off this thing, but then I met Rebecca in January (2003).

Put simply, she was genuine, down to earth, good fun and what I needed in that she was non-Luton related and a good listener, even when she overheard a personal phone call from an employed student who saw fit to phone and behave like a fish-wife down the phone. It was that bad. We quickly gave each other nicknames and got on well, spending more and more time together, which faded Luton into a thankful background. Something was more important than work and it was not an obsession with getting to Northern Ireland games.

Of course, that was still the number one hobby and I explained this from the off. Rebecca was ·responsive suggesting that if things got serious, she would keep out of the way, as sport, save an occasional day on the booze at the cricket was not her scene. This was a great response, as I did not need to use the 'working away' excuse or whatever when Northern Ireland played abroad. Moreover, she now books my hotel rooms, as she works for Hilton Group, at the favourable rate of around £20 per person per night, for five star opulence. It's no wonder Robert Walsh leaves the bookings to me.

The first game in the period of our relationship was a February friendly with Finland at Windsor Park. After the last fixture against Finland in late 1999 I had my 'Lawrie Out Shaun In!' decision, but this time I was looking for a goal, as a year had passed since the Poland game.

However, prior to the game I was carrying out a promise to Auntie Barbara and carrying out some rare diplomatic family business. She had asked me, off the record, if I would visit her other (full) brother Jimmy, in Enniskillen, some time when I was in the province in the hope that there could be some family reconciliation and all three children could perhaps be together one last time, as none of them were getting any younger. This was a very reasonable request, as Barbara was 70, and she felt it was time to bury any hatchets.

Dad travels to Northern Ireland regularly for motorbike meetings such as the 'NorthWest 200' festival meeting in May, but never drops by his brother, even though he holiday's for at least a week on the island. I once asked why and was dealt the frosty response that, 'I asked him to be my best man and he said 'No', so as far as I am concerned bollocks to him'. Bearing that in mind I anticipated that 'Challenge Shaun' would be a difficult one, more like Mission Impossible, but I did as requested. I found the their property, backing on to the local golf course, and met Jimmy's wife at the door, who to her credit vaguely recognised a person she had not seen since the early 80's, when they visited us at the family home. She called her husband who responded from upstairs saying, 'Fine! I will just finish my painting job' and he arrived some fifteen minutes later. We did the niceties and parted on amicable terms, but I knew this was not going to work, and e-mailed Barbara on the return home. Latterly I told Mum and Dad I did this, and Dad said, 'That sums him up!' No love lost there then, similar to my elder sister and me, but not quite as acute. At least we speak, though similarly we are not on each other's Christmas card list.

I journeyed back to Belfast feeling happy I had done this task and was disturbed by Leslie, who said she had some important news and NOT to be late into the pub, which had had a make-over, transforming into the trendy Vaughan's bar and losing half the bar staff.

This doesn't please many, in the least Paul, Leslie's then boyfriend, who arrives from work and needs a drink, or several, some say to numb the feeling of watching Northern Ireland. I say 'then boyfriend' because Leslie announced that they were to marry in October, but not to announce it wildly, particularly to IFA staff.

As for the game, I have previously explained spectating in high summer's balmy evenings or during the harshest autumn tempest. On this occasion fog reared its bizarre head. For some reason I can remember an England v Bulgaria game in the late 70s being cancelled for one day because of fog, but this was the real thing. Officially the rule is that a game can be abandoned if both goals cannot be seen from the halfway line, and though was the case on numerous brief occasions; the fog never reached this density for long periods. We were watching from the side of the pitch, but there was no way anyone in the Spion Kop could see what was going on, but maybe this was no bad thing as Northern Ireland leaked to Liverpool's Sammi Hyppia early in the second half and lost 0-1. His Finnish teamates had requested the game abandoned at half time, but to no avail and I cheekily asked David Currie if there was a refund for sight restrictive seats! 'No', was the typically mild reply, as we shook hands outside the ground and mutually said 'See you in Armenia'.

This is an often bizarre comment made between the supporters and administrators, who have no communication, save occasional e-mail and phone conversations, and never see each other except around the world at football internationals.

ARMENIA STOOD STILL

I had first met David Currie on the charter trip to Armenia in 1997 and six years later we were both returning albeit via different ways. Air travel has evolved to an extent that Austrian Airlines tend to be the option to such far off lands, though some supporters and the team took the occasional direct British Airways route. Robert and I took the former, arriving at Yerevan in the dead of night and I immediately noticed on disembarking that nothing had changed, from the bland concrete, to the light fittings hanging off from the ceiling to that common East European smell of rotting garbage and blocked drains.

As for the hotel, the owner had promised to collect us from the airport given the arrival time. Sure enough the patron of the Hotel Areg was waiting holding up one of those peculiar 'welcome to our country signs', which doubled as a piece of A4 with Schofield on. I had booked the Hotel Areg on Christmas Day, having being more than a little bored with James Bond and my elder sister talking the ruby port to a standstill. I simply put 'hotels in Yerevan' into Google, found a listing and booked the first one, as it was in the city and pretty cheap at $18 a night each. On Boxing Day, a Mr. Petrosyan confirmed the booking offering the said pickup.

What turned out to be Mr. Petrosyan and his friend bundled Robert and I into the back of an old BMW 3series saloon and whisked us into Yerevan, but with hindsight it could have been anywhere.

Weaving from side to side to avoid the potholes (nothing had changed) on the pitch black dual carriageway, a regular trait given the electric shortage, we were taken to the hotel but we shared a fear that this guy could be a mafia front and merely taking us to the forest, robbing us bare and getting his kids into university. It literally had that 'Wild West' feel, compounded by the fact that on arrival we were stripped of passports and sent to ice cold rooms via a lift which took us to the fourth floor, even though the top floor button, which was our floor, had 9 on it!

Neither of us slept well and the shower was cold in this 'budget style' hotel, but we needn't have worried because in the cold light of a freezing Yerevan morning we were extended a warm greeting by family Petrosyan once they had received their dollars. Robert took the peppered egg breakfast, to which my stomach was turning, and then the service began. Service in that anything we wanted we got from friends taxis to beer for breakfast, to extra blankets. I am convinced the hoteliers had never had Western guests and did all they could for us, in this converted house in a very deprived neighbourhood with open drains and ditches. Our currency was even paying for an extension, for on returning from the Under-21s game, huge piles of sand and rubble were outside. We asked Mr. Petrosyan about this and he said it was paid for by our dollars as the Armenian had a no credit economy. He went on to explain in stunted English that you had 'made it' in Armenia if you were on the capitalist ladder and owned a kiosk. These are literally everywhere in places like Yerevan, selling mostly convenience goods, like toothpaste and crisps to half drunk foreigners like myself, but unfortunately the owners tend also to live in the back of these kiosks. It is everything they own and quite a sad sight seeing a middle aged man available 24/7, just in case someone needs something, unlike in France, where every persons dream is to become a civil servant 'functionaire' and retire on a state pension at 55.

Our morning taxi took us downtown, where we bumped into David Currie and Derek McKinley who told us to get to their hotel for 1.45 pm coach trip to the Under21 game in Abovyan.

On board, someone asked Malcolm Brodie what had changed in the last seven years, to which he replied 'Nothing. Absolutely nothing.' My mentioned view compounded, the coach took us into the hills and through snow storms and all to the most decrepit football ground I have ever seen. The toilet, yes the single toilet, was a sewer without running water and the ground just a bowl with horizontal iron railings for seating: the whole place summing up the abject poverty which Armenia has to live with.

One ray of brightness was the Amalgamation Supporters visiting an orphanage with bags of clothes and goodies along with Embassy and media support. I raided the Student Union freebie cupboard and took T-shirts emblazoned with Coca-Cola and Robert took drawing kits, which were much appreciated, but I find it annoying to see people looking for gifts, looking hungry and much older than their years, whilst money is poured into a new model national stadium.

The Under 21 game was suspended for an hour due to a snow storm and the inevitable snow ball fight between visiting supporters AND the team who had fresh supplies on the pitch as they warmed up. The surrealism was complete when the pitch was remarked in blue and a dark blue ball was used for the game, as the winter sun melted the snow and the pitch developed into a quagmire. The team lost 0-2.

The bizarreness of this trip continued into the evening as Robert and me ended up in the team hotel for a drink, for no other reason that it was warm and there may be some chat and hospitality. I had looked at the Hyatt hotel on the net with a view to booking, but felt $180 a night each was a rip-off, and settled on the Areg at 15% of the price!

I deduce that tourist executive hotels are all the same and you could be in Moscow, Copenhagen or wherever in these places and the money spent on a room for the night is far more important to a guy making his way in the world than a grey-suited accountant in an office calculating occupancy rates and cumulative room spend! (Hilton's excepted).

Nevertheless it was not long before Jim Boyce, Derek McKinley, David Currie and Under-21 official Glenda Dines came by to say hello and share tales of the Abovyan experience. Similarly BBC Ulster's Jackie Fullerton came by asking, 'Are you two here for the game!', to which we said 'Yes', but only because we could not think of anything more ridiculous to say. Then not once, but twice, Sammy McIlroy, came to sit with us and literally poured his heart to us, in an almost valedictory way.

He seemed genuinely upset that players had not travelled, for reasons as varied as Yerevan being only 500 miles from the new war-zone in Iraq and the more usual and seemingly spurious excuse of injury. His parting remark was 'I hope whoever takes over from me does not get the same…', which smacked of hopelessness and an inability to make his feelings known to the press, who would not doubt seize on his thoughts with their usual gusto. Robert and me were initially gobsmacked, but quickly began to pick over McIlroy's thoughts deducing that he had taken Northern Ireland as far as he could and wanted to walk away from a team who were not confident and not scored for over a year. We decided he would probably resign after the Greece game the following Wednesday and felt as a gesture of goodwill to McIlroy would keep our conversation strictly confidential.

As mentioned, the match took place in the new national stadium, and Northern Ireland fell to a break away sucker punch three minutes from time, after having dominated for long periods, particularly late in the first half when they somehow conspired not to score a goal, when netting was an easier option. I got on my hobby horse as some supporters, no doubt the worse for wear as vodka was 50p a bottle, booed the team and faced my wrath, but it did not matter what we did, as the die was cast and the 0-1 scoreline was the result.

Dejectedly we walked back to the town centre, hitting on a stylish restaurant, complete with an English menu, which is imperative in countries whose alphabet is not even in the same language and food may be as varied as sheep brain or dog. The hosts were most courteous, particularly as I needed the toilet to wash away the staining green face paint and as we were seated a man on the other table explained in perfect English that he was (sarcastically) sad that we had come many a mile to see Northern Ireland. Suggesting it was water off a duck's back we enquired who, what, where this man was from.

He gave us a card, said he was from Manchester and had a business interest in Yerevan and invited us to meet him for coffee the following lunchtime at said premises. We agreed, much out of curiosity, but not before he had left us a surprise for after dinner.

After the meal, a waiter arrived with a bottle of chilled vodka and two shot glasses and we were told Mani had left it for us. Genially, though I hate the very thought of vodka, we filled the glasses and had a slug, replaced the cap and retired to the bar for the local Zamelek beer, which was disgusting on Friday morning, but now after a few, had a more pleasant taste, given taste buds short term memory loss for the likes of Stella. A waiter followed us with said bottle of vodka, and insisted it was ours, but we retorted saying it was fine and we had had a glass. His manager arrived and explained the whole bottle was ours for the drinking and was a usual after dinner scenario, akin to brandy and cigars. This was now the famed (Russian/East European) hospitality coming to the fore, but a bottle of vodka was not on our radar and we gave it to the staff, albeit a little embarrassingly.

On Sunday lunchtime, Mani explained his business in Armenia, which was as an exporter of British DIY tools to his homeland. He suggested there was a market for it among the rich in Yerevan, but his business was non-profit making and more of a welfare front for the staff he employed, as it was a way of feeding a dozen families. He then went on to explain the desperate straits many found themselves in Yerevan, with doctors and nurses unpaid for months on end, horrendous housing conditions and people literally doing anything to get bread on the table.

Looking out of his office window compounded his view, with an earthquake (in 1989) damaged inhabited high-rise block, circled by rotting rubbish and festering dogs. It was depressing in the extreme, particularly as children were using the rubbish tip as a playground. Mani said the flats inside were OK by and large as this was often all the inhabitants had materialistically, and was a gift from the overthrow of communism's 'living space for all' policy.

Any unwanted goods though went to market in an attempt to make a few dollars, which was situated an old communist style concrete fountain style park, and Sunday afternoon saw the flea market to end all flea markets. It had everything from radio and car parts to Soviet military hats to tablecloths to Soviet bank notes. Our mistake was to buy a Soviet military cap from one of the first stalls on the market. Simply, dollars were exchanged and thereafter we had all kind of hawkers following Uncle Sam's smell, one such person, a little old lady selling lace, following us for an hour slowly devaluing her wares in the hope of a sale. Eventually we gave her a dollar; her need greater than mine for a beer in a Western style bar.

The depressing reality of life, everyday Armenian style, made me think politically and conclude that were the average Britons wrong to decry asylum seekers wanting to better their life economically by stowing away in a truck for days at a time and ultimately flipping burgers or frying chicken in a downtown English inner-city. Seven hours work at £5 an hour is a king's ransom to these poor souls and I would suggest a radical plan would be to import such labour and export to Armenia the benefit loving underbelly of British society who spuriously drain our nation of resources and then add to the profits of the local pub and bookmaker. They would soon learn about poverty, depression and hard luck stories. One could perhaps see how angry I felt about seeing these people existing in this manner to feed themselves. It was just not right, nor was the outward opulence that the more fortunate Armenians wallowed in with their black Mercedes cars and designer suits, which Robert and me saw later that evening.

The main square in Yerevan consists of four corners: a bank, a post office (and they never did send the cards), the refurbished, but then closed, Hotel Yerevan, where I stayed in 1997, and finally a small parade of designer shops with an underground restaurant. I looked into the restaurant and saw crisp table linen, numerous wine glasses and polished cutlery laid on each table and suggested to Robert we 'dress-up' (ie not in football kit) and dine out Armenian style, to which he agreed, using the reason that if we spend a load of money in this restaurant, it might help pay a few wages.

Arriving at 8.00 p.m, we were harshly escorted to another part of the building with an annexed restaurant. I explained we wanted the 'posh' place and the escort said we had to eat here. I was curious and went to the real restaurant with my camera, as I wanted to take a photo of this Ritz type place. I gently opened the glass fronted door to be met by a gun carrying male in KGB style leather trench coat. He gestured me to leave without speaking and being the compliant type with gun holders bade a hasty retreat, latterly finding out the President of Armenia was dining with a few guests!

More guns were on display in security guards holsters at the airport the following morning, to which Mr.

Petrosyan escorted us to at 3.00 a.m., for our flight to Vienna, but not before a convenient exit visa salesman charged us $20 to leave. I must be one of only a few people around who have two stamps in their passport to Armenia, but this one was a relieved one, as Yerevan airport is not for the faint hearted at any time, particularly at night as its broken escalators, radiators and light fittings give you a feeling that you are on a Scooby-Doo cartoon set. Thank-you, goodbye, and here's to the next time!

THE ICE MAN COMETH

The press at home had obviously not got wind of Sammy McIlroy's feelings, as he was getting his squad 'up' for the Greece game on the Wednesday night in Belfast.

I was naturally travelling via Luton (well every cloud has a silver lining) to the match, and had a rare companion in tow. I mentioned earlier that many say they want to go to Belfast to watch football, but nobody, save David in Calais had done so. The next exception was a guy called Ominarios Fantarios, or ICE for short. Ice, nicknamed for simplistic reasons and the fact he drank copious amounts of Smirnoff Ice, which had incidentally just been launched on draught in Northern Ireland, was a sabbatical officer at University of Luton. These are paid positions involving some modicum of responsibility, but are often used as an excuse to put off the need to find gainful employment and enjoy another year drinking cheap booze with a student card. Ice's remit was student welfare and he did carry out the job responsibly, but personally he was Greek; hence his request for a trip to Belfast, with Leslie guaranteeing his ticket as part of her allocation of four.

Roy and Tim Glover, another member of the Silver Band, had arranged lunch in the Quality Hotel, and took great pleasure in entertaining Ice, who did not need a second opportunity to fill his belly, weighing in at twenty stone and being the mainstay of the Stockwood Park Rugby Club front row.

I have always found this trait a most enjoyable one amongst the people of Northern Ireland, who extend their hospitality, as explained, far beyond the front door to any 'foreigner'. As for Ice, he could not believe the hospitality or the tastiness of the locally caught fish (and chips) and it was not long before he was matching Tim and Roy, Guinness for Guinness. Personally, I am always perplexed by the locals who say on departing, even if it's just to join others company, 'Thanks for coming"! I get the feeling it may be a throw back to the days of 'The Troubles', when visitors and certainly tourists were probably few and far between and a strange face, if not viewed with suspicion, was seen as someone who could spread the positive vibes of Northern Ireland. Certainly Rebecca, on her first visit was more than impressed with the hospitality, architecture, scenery and tranquillity of Ulster's countryside on her first visit in October 2003.

By kick-off time Ice, was certainly the worst for wear, having visited other famous Belfast hostelries, including Robinson's and The Crown on Great Victoria Street and getting into a session with Lesley's boyfriend Paul in Hunter's. Certainly his rendition of the Greek national anthem was distinctly off-key, as probably was mine of God Save The Queen, as I suffered the embarrassment of falling (drunkenly) 'up' the stairs in the South Stand, as I visited the toilet. Of course, Northern Ireland lost the game 0-2, much to Ice's delight, but news from David Currie part way through the game, diverted my attention away from a poor performance.

Northern Ireland's next fixture was a prestige fixture against Italy in early June, for which I had booked a BA flight to Naples; leaving on Tuesday afternoon and returning on Thursday morning. However, as the game was a friendly, the Italian FA decided to re-arrange the match to the Tuesday night. With the fixture venue being Campobasso, a large town in central Southern Italy, two hours car (hire) drive from Naples, I had no alternative but to tear up my travel plans and airline ticket and start again.

It is situations like this that really wind me, and no doubt countless others who deal with the travel industry, up, in that when I contacted BA, asking if I could change my plans or just use the return ticket, I just got a 'NO, NO, NO', with the inference being that they have got the money, and if you don't want to use the service then tough luck! Appalling customer service, but something, to their credit, flag carrying airlines are working on, as the budget airlines stake their reputations on cost effective flexibility. For the trip, I eventually used a return flight via Easyjet, whom have saved me countless hundreds of pounds in travel to and from Belfast since they launched their service in 1999.

At the end of the Greece game, I had an appointment with David Healy, who true to his word, despite pressure from other supporters, promised me his match shirt, following a chance meeting with him and Stephen Lomas in Yerevan. As we sit in the South Stand, which houses the team changing rooms and the various match officials, I often, with John and Gavin, catch a word with the Healy family and other players as they depart. As such, I do consider I can approach Healy as a known face, hence my asking for the shirt. These are a rare currency, as international strips are generally engraved with the match and date and are authentic to collectors. I simply wanted one to wear and Healy obliged on the proviso that I made a donation to a charity of my choice. As my niece is a special needs child, a charity which provides wishes for sick children such as Lapland visits to see Santa Claus had their coffers swelled and everyone was a winner: except Ice though, who needed two days off after the visit to get his head together!

I'VE GOT MIRRORS THANK GOD

As intimated, I was annoyed by BA's attitude and for the record I have yet to find another industry, save hotels, who oversell capacity quite purposely in the HOPE that everybody does not show up. Easyjet state they do not do this, and there were naturally two seats for Robert and me on a flight from Stansted. We hooked up with Gavin Lavery in the airport lobby in Naples and then took control of our transport to Campobasso: a Fiat Punto. Public transport was a non-starter as trains were difficult; hence I was putting our destiny behind a steering wheel. Driving in Naples is all you hear about, with most cars either dented or scratched and everyone trying to get to destination before the car in front at any cost. Coupled to the fact we hadn't a clue where the road to Campobasso began a recipe for a lost car deposit was in the offing.

We found our way onto a motorway with signs for Rome to which Robert exclaimed, 'Fu** me! We're in the outside lane doing 140!' This is rare for Robert who doesn't often vent his feelings and has a quiet voice. However, shortly after we saw a sign for Campobasso and just headed for it, not caring if it was via Rome, Brussels or London: the relief being most welcome.

The Italy versus Northern Ireland match up was a kind of benefit game, with the Azzuri visiting this outpost to show support for the locals who had suffered earthquake damage and minor loss of life earlier in the year. This could be seen by cracks in buildings, motorway bridges and the like. Indeed, supporters' clubs officials Jim Rainey and Alan Ferris were seen giving a cheque for 3,000Euros to the local relief fund.

Now Northern Ireland away support is more organised and plentiful, I find these gestures (like the one in Armenia) most pleasant, simply because it shows supporters simply for what we all should be: caring human beings helping the less fortunate. Whether or not gestures like this 'friendly' up the rivalry between supporters is debatable, but the green of Northern Ireland always get a welcome wherever it is, unlike the fear and hate often reported when England are in town. I garbed myself up in green, with wig, face paint and all for this game and had many Italian youngsters wanting a photo call, with even one wanting an autograph! Also the fact, my wardrobe is full of opposition scarves, which are merely decorative for supporters rather than weather functional, suggests people in foreign lands are genuine in welcoming Northern Ireland. I just hope Jim's gestures of charity do make that little difference.

Once inside the ground, the Tifosi (Italian supporters) seemed bemused that some 200 away supporters were humming and conducting the Italian anthem, made famous on these shores no doubt by the exploits of the Ferrari Formula One team (both the winning car and driver have the anthem played), but once down to business on the pitch, the game was almost a mirror image of the 1997 Sicily affair, with Northern Ireland defending for long periods, only occasionally breaking out, but threatening little and losing 2-0. There was a sea change in the Northern Ireland squad though, with a set of new kids on the block getting a run out in Tommy Docherty, Andy Smith and Gary Hamilton, who was plying his trade with Northern Ireland part-timers Portadown. As for Italy, they got their run out against British opposition, with an important 'must-win' Euro fixture against Wales shortly to follow, who had beaten them in Cardiff the previous autumn allowing the Welsh team to wallow in, and dine-out on the myth that they were a good side.

Robert had to be back at the airport for an 11.00 a.m. flight, which meant no night out in Campobasso, which hardly rancoured as there was nothing there save the ubiquitous Irish bar and a taxi service run by the local red cross operation, but it left Gavin and me in Naples for a day.

I am none too keen on the tourist trail, but Gavin persuaded me to take a trip to Sorrento, across the bay of Naples, past Vesuvius and Pompeii, and playground of both tourists and the Italian rich. I have to say begrudgingly that I did like this day out, not least because I ate my way around the town via the ice-cream parlours! If it's a choice of a day on the piss, or a day on the ice cream or cakes, I would succumb to the latter, as David in Calais would testify, as I would gauge our days out in France or Belgium on the standard of the localities' bakeries. A bit sad I know, but that's the way to this adopted Northern Ireland supporters' heart, as the saying goes!

Before my attention turned to the international cricket season, Northern Ireland had a Euro fixture to complete against Spain in Belfast the following Wednesday, which was a worry as Northern Ireland had lost 0-5 the previous spring and 0-3 in autumn and Sammy McIlroy had decided to stick with the young guns who had been spirited in defeat against the Italians.

The atmosphere prior to the game was bizarre: a kind of resignation over the forthcoming result combined with a garden party/valedictory summer ball atmosphere in that the sun was shining and the alcohol flowing.

Except for Alan Ferris and Paul Russell that is: the former who could not get into the snooker club on the Lisburn Road for a drink and the latter who could neither get served in Hunter's OR the local off-licence! Disaster! Paul was sober on entry to the ground, but as for Hunter's (or Vaughan's in its present carnation) they do themselves no favours. Surely the pub nearest the ground should be set up for a rush, but they persist in having six bar staff on duty to serve what seems like most of Belfast, who get racked off when the wait us upwards of twenty minutes!

Whether sober or not, supporters were in for a pleasant surprise on the pitch as McIlroy's young guns held Spain to a deserved 0-0 draw, going close to shocking Raul, Baraja, Morientes et al on at least two occasions. Such a performance made the garden party atmosphere even more palatable as goodbyes were said, coupled to 'see you in September'.

I always find this scenario quite amusing, as you know the people you sit around through football and often little else. For 90 minutes of a match you are like a blood brother and so close, but other than that you rarely see them, don't even know where they live, probably do not know their surname and certainly do not exchange Christmas cards. For example, I bump into Alan Ferris and Lesley's husband at every home game, but know little else about them (though I know Paul very well now) save they breathe the same air and watch Northern Ireland!

AN AWAY AWAY MATCH

Northern Ireland chose not to use the August friendly date, instead concentrating their (and supporters) minds on the arduous trip to Ukraine in September. Instead Gavin (Lavery) and me decided to adopt a 'second' team for a few days and ended up in Denmark for their friendly with Finland, which came with an added bonus.

Rebecca had taken up a job with Ladbrokes, which are part of Hilton group and she had delved into the company perks situation and come up with the notion that any Ladbrokes employee, subject to availability, could book a Hilton for £20 (or equivalent) a night inclusive of breakfast. Kastrup Airport Hilton duly obliged and we stayed in this ultra modern complex, complete with Bang and Oulfsen gadgetry.

Majbritt had 'sold' Denmark to me in 2001, and I still hanker for an migratory move there, but throughout the break I was distracted by the forthcoming Ukraine trip. I had to get my passport to a West End Travel agents' house on return from Denmark and hope it would be added to the group visa, as Robert and me had booked to fly to Donetsk on the team charter flight, which was taking thirty selected supporters. Ultimately, there was no problem with this, but the fact Ukraine had decided to play this game in quite inaccessible Eastern Ukraine, showed how difficult the Ukrainians could play international football politics.

In friendly fixtures, where an invitation to play is in the offing, the hosts often pay hotel and/or travel expenses, as occurred when Northern Ireland got a huge bill after world champions France visited in 1999. However, in qualifying fixtures respective teams pay their own way and in this case, it necessitated a £75,000 charter flight.

Donetsk is Ukraine's second city and politically aligned towards the traditional hand of control from 'mother Russia', unlike the West of the country, including Kiev, which sees itself as a liberal free-market society neighbouring the EU. Not withstanding, Donetsk is fiercely nationalistic, and perhaps an ideal place to play an all important qualifying game, though not, as explained for travelling purposes. It is also the home of Shaktar Donetsk, a rising light in European football, rivalling once all-conquering Dinamo Kiev for Ukrainian supremacy, and who had once made life difficult for Arsenal in the Champions League. This is due in the main to a Ukrainian, Roman Abramovich style owner, who has pumped millions of dollars into his Donetsk plaything.

On first sight though, it was a pity he had not pumped any money into the airport; a grey communist throw back complete with rusting Soviet Tuplolev's near the runway, suspicious border guards and pre-fabricated dimly lit cardboard entry booths.

An hour after passing through and crammed literally into two supporters mini-buses, we were whisked to the hotel: the main topic of conversation not so much being the social deprivation but whether a mooted Caribbean tour next summer would come to fruition. Apparently Jim Boyce had met up, at a FIFA event, with Caribbean football's 'Mr-Big', Jack Walker, and after discussing cricket for some time had moved on to football and he had literally invited the Northern Ireland team over to the West Indies, with fixtures against Trinidad, Jamaica and St. Kitts very much on the agenda. Personally, I do not like hot weather, obviously synonymous with the Caribbean, but me and Robert struck up a deal on the mini-bus, that we would go, come what may.

To the business in hand, we eventually checked into the hotel, whose name I can still not remember, after much form filling and paper-stamping: a popular trait in (far) Eastern Europe. This is because in Communist times it gave people something to do and a wage, and was particularly prevalent here and Moldova, where I had a bus ticket clipped and stamped by two separate people. Here the time wasting incorporated a concierge stamping our hotel booking docket as we came to and from our third floor penthouse room complete with balcony.

A Thursday night out in downtown Donetsk proved to be a bit of a damp squib, save the bar opposite the hotel by the cinema, which had run out of lager by match day Saturday afternoon as it became the supporters official hostelry, and we took an early night complete with dinner, comprising of Ritz crackers and Cheetos. Cheetos are like continental Wotsits, quite disgusting and make you belch all night, but it is surprising how often these turn up when food is required, simply because you know what they are, harmless and have a packet with writing on that you can understand. In this land of backward Es and upturned Rs, this can often be quite comforting, as can the golden arches of McDonalds.

A Friday morning jaunt via a bank exchanging dollars for (Ukrainian) hrvana and a fly ridden, bad smelling food market selling raw, unchilled meat and fish ultimately revealed a McDonalds, to which Robert said 'Right! That'll do me!' I didn't argue either, but I did think, albeit briefly as hunger pains took over, what a hypocrite I was. In the West, I refuse to visit McDonalds, save for their spotlessly clean toilet, as I simply believe the food to be tasteless and unhealthy, but here, as in Romania and Moldova, it is part of the traveller's essential kit. This is because, no matter what kind of stomach upsetting stuff goes in a burger, you know it's likely to be the same everywhere and shouldn't harm you, save a bad pooh or two. Eating local food can have the opposite effect, and having seen a tramp styled woman making chips with a butter knife in a Yerevan pizza restaurant, I suggest my opinion on local food is correct.

However, save for McDonalds, a KFC and an Irish bar where the Shankill supporters were feeding, Donetsk in my opinion is a tourist's paradise, in that it is so totally different from the straight jacketed norm of a city centre. For example, the same shops dominate malls in Paris, Amsterdam, London et al: the only difference being their different respective monuments being sold in the same Chinese made snowstorms. Here this was certainly not the case, with a statue of Lenin dominating the town's main square and no Japanese tourists clicking away or recording with the latest digi-equipment. It seemed bizarrely strange, but I liked it: a place where there were no tourists, like Hanki's town in northern Czech, where people were just getting on with their lives, without Westernized trappings.

In the Irish pub, I asked the bar person why Lenin was still around. In her perfect no-slang, non dialect English, she said he was once their leader, for right or wrong and should be remembered. Whether 60ft of remembrance was really necessary is questionable, but what else could be put there. With hindsight, I remembered in Kiev in 1997, that I had seen statues of Stalin and Lenin, but they were very much tucked away in a park. I did express an interest in what the bar person had to say, because bizarrely it is a wish of mine to meet one of these feared (and revered) leaders, be it Lenin, Hitler, Honecker, or more potently, as North Korea still exists as a Stalinist utopia, Kim Jon-Il. Simply, I would just like to know what makes them tick.

A trip of this nature has its benefits in that I got a rare opportunity to see the Under-21s game, with numerous other supporters, Jim Rainey and Marty included, who had arrived on the so-called 'party-train' from Kiev. As space on the charter was limited, other supporters had flown to Kiev, and taken an overnight train eastwards,swelling the travelling ranks to around 50. To the bemusement of the locals, songs, such as 'Party-Train...reeling and rocking' and 'Woo... We're going to Barbados' rang out from the stands in between a conga and a request for Glenda Dines to give us a wave! It was quite surreal, but the team still lost 0-1.

Of course the geography of Donetsk to Britain makes travel expensive, but once there the saving grace is that things are cheap (and women beautiful and they know it) with vodka retailing at the same price as a bottle of beer at 50p a half litre. Safe to assume therefore that a good night out was had by all, particularly Robert, whom I carried back to the hotel from the downtown Biker's Bar, at a ridiculously early 11p.m.

However, this did not augur well for the supporters match the following morning.

I played, or rather attempted to play, in one of these against a German team in Belfast in 1997 and have never worn football boots since. If three wishes are ever to be granted to me by a fairy godmother, one would be to draw caricatures, another would be to jam a saxophone Lisa Simpson style, and finally I would like to be able to play football to reasonable standard. Not international class, but good enough to perhaps play on a Sunday morning.

This time, numerous inebriated supporters arrived in taxis to attempt to play against a group of Ukrainian supporters on what I believe was Shaktar's training ground. Save to say the standard was not good, but Alan and Jim, could quite clearly hold their own. Others were playing as rolling substitutes, as Friday night's alcohol and years of bodily neglect meant little more than a gentle trot could be mustered most of the time. Personally, I felt quite proud that I was playing in a green strip for Northern Ireland and more so that I somehow got the ball to Jim Rainey who scored the winning goal in this

6-5 thriller. It was all good fun, but many suffered from sport induced asthma, myself included, whilst others, including Darren from the IFA were just sick!

At the full international, one chant spoke of Rainey's spectacular suggesting, 'Who put the ball in the Ukraine net...super Jimmy Rainey.' However, the main event of the evening, as far as Northern Ireland's supporters were concerned, came around half an hour into the game. This was the moment, Jim McComish, a supporter from a Stourbridge, had calculated as being the 1000th minute since Northern Ireland last scored. The moment was greeted by a 60 second countdown and a chorus based on the Proclaimers '500Miles' song, with supporters waiting (at least) 1000 minutes to watch Northern Ireland score. At least we, the supporters found the funny side!

Unsurprisingly Northern Ireland did not score, but nor did Ukraine, and the 0-0 result left their hopes of a trip to Portugal the following summer in tatters. The group had been a tight one at the top, with Spain, Greece and Ukraine vying for the qualifying spots. Spain had lost to Greece earlier in the campaign and were fighting Ukraine for second place, but this result in Donetsk effectively ended Ukrainian hopes. To their credit, Northern Ireland continued their battling spirit, noticeable in the Spain game, and though not particularly pretty it was effective. Still, as the pundits say, if you want aesthetics, go and watch ice-skating! McIlroy seemed pleased, as we queued to clear customs, suggesting that in two years time this squad would really develop and be a match for anyone. Certainly, there was a spirit amongst the youngsters who seemed eager to perform and the flight home was buoyed with optimism, as Northern Ireland were to play Armenia the following Wednesday night, and all were looking for a positive result against moderate opposition.

Whilst moderate, Armenia could also be considered as a 'nuisance value' team, in that their geographical proximity means it will always be a difficult place to travel to and get a result, and when on their travels they have enough savvy to frustrate an occasional result out of superior opposition. I suppose the same could be said about Northern Ireland, as both Spain and Ukraine found out and perhaps this fixture could be termed 'the nuisance encounter', with only pride between the teams being at stake.

It turned out not to be a 'nuisance', but a downright disaster as Northern Ireland succumbed 0-1. I suppose this could be seen as a cyclical disaster to parallel the events against Albania and Latvia in times gone by, but the hope in the airport from four days previously now became open despair. As for not scoring, Gavin Nixon said 'I don't want us to score. We've come this bloody far without scoring; we might has well go through the whole lot.' Clarke Gibson queried the 'no-refund' policy, suggesting if this performance was purchased from Tesco, a refund would be in the offing. It was that bad! I felt totally dejected, knowing that people would happily rip the piss out of me over this. Yes, they did and though battle hardened over this kind of result, it was the display that I just could not stomach. I could have walked away from this journey then, but after doing it for eight years thought 'Hey! What the hell else would I spend my money on?' I certainly wasn't McMenemyesque and was looking forward over the next couple of weeks to the Greece game and another encounter with Ice.

DAY TRIP TO ATHENS WITH ICE

This took place on the second Saturday in October and travel wise was a perfect way to end the qualifying series, with a little late warm autumn sunshine and the sights of Athens. However, I was busy at work, early into a new academic year of plying attitude-ridden students with cheap booze and then cleaning up the mess, which necessitated a day trip. This was a pity as Ice had moved back to Greece, to start his (desk-job) national service and invited me to spend some time at his hospitality. Many others though, not least the Carrickfergus Silver Band contingent, including Crewe based Paul Shanks and the aptly named Pancake (as his birthday is apparently near Shrove Tuesday) enjoyed Ice hosting them around the country and various islands. His worth was also most merited at the Under 21 game, when he negotiated ground entry and exit with the local police.

He was also there to meet at Athens airport and quickly whisked me off to a very social afternoon in various tavernas which Roy and Tim had quickly got to know.

The game was played in the Olyimpiakos stadium, rather than the National/Olympic Stadium, which was being rebuilt for the forthcoming Olympiad. It was a 15,000 capacity football stadium, rather than a complex ground with a running track perimeter, which meant for a great atmosphere, particularly as the Greek supporters in each 'end' tried to out-shout each other. This scenario is typical in many grounds, especially in Southern Europe, whereas the Northern Ireland supporters were chanting about Roy Millar being on the dole. Millar was responsible for the Under21 team, which was being (temporarily as it turned out) wound up after this fixture, due to financial constraints, but the song was nothing if not amusing.

The Greeks had already qualified, whether directly or by the play-off for second place, for the next phase, and the home supporters were in a party mood, supplanted by their routine 1-0 victory. The goal came via a penalty following George McCartney's 'last-man in the box' foul, for which he was red carded. Ice was ecstatic, but did not show it, as he was then surrounded by two hundred plus travelling supporters, though the drinks were certainly on him later.

Everyone else was simply 'resigned' to the normal 0 against the country's name and was somewhat dumb-founded as news filtered around the faithful that McIlroy had been offered a two year extension to his contract.

However, I personally was not surprised when it did not come to pass and he resigned his position shortly after the Greek game, returning to club football with Stockport County. His comments in Armenia and latterly in the customs queue in Donetsk airport made sense now and it his perhaps to his credit that he at least saw his job with Northern Ireland through to a logical end at a qualifying series conclusion. Sure he pressed the right buttons in his valedictory departure, suggesting he missed day-to-day interaction with footballers, rather than for 4 weeks a year, but for me his mind was made up that Friday night in Yerevan. As someone who has had to learn time management I counter his opinion saying that someone in his position should, after 3 years, know how to efficiently use his time.

To his credit, McIlroy also developed and blooded the likes of Healy, Jones, McCartney and others, countering the 'retirement' of Magilton, Taggert and Lennon, but with hindsight I, like most others, think his departure was for the best. Some have suggested his defensive record, in that Northern Ireland only conceded eight goals in this qualifying series, was commendable, but the cold facts that Northern Ireland lost to Armenia (twice) and could not beat Liechtenstein or Cyprus and did not score for his final 1140 odd minutes in charge, meant he had to go.

As it was termed and chanted, 'Sammy McIlroy's Green and White Army' lost its leader, but back to the present, a night out in Athens was in the offing.

This was going to be a personal trial, due to my travel logistics. Finishing work at 2am on Saturday morning, I bussed and tubed to Heathrow for a 7.30 a.m. flight. A two hour time addition and three and half hour flight meant the liaison with Ice at 1.30 p.m. as completed without sleep, as I find it hard to more than doze on an plane, given the clank of trolleys, the all too common screaming child and the general discomfort of aeroplane seats. As such, I was without sleep, and it was after 3am on the morning following the game when I finally saw the interior of my eyelids. Ice had booked his favourite taverna for a party after the game; a superb gesture, and the wine, beer and ouzo flowed, along with the most divine and calorific fried feta cheese, which only exacerbated my sleep deficit. Indeed on occasions like this, I often wonder why I ever booked a hotel room. A couch in a lobby, or even grass under a tree in a park would have done the trick on this occasion, and saved me £30 for the four hours sleep I had. For the record, I cannot even remember getting to the hotel, where it was or what it was called. Ice must have been a great host, or I was tired, or both!

WHERE DO WE GO FROM HERE?

Following McIlroy's departure, IFA officials had a double dilemma. One was who to appoint as manager, who could keep both the support of the growing army of supporters and resurrect Northern Ireland's rapidly fading beacon; remembering the fourth oldest national association's team had qualified for the World Cup only 17 years previously and now were no match for Armenia. Secondly, a World Cup qualifying draw was coming up in Germany in December and there was nobody in place to represent and plot a qualifying campaign.

The plus side was that Northern Ireland were taking a break from international football and had four months before a proposed friendly against Norway in February to sort out the manager's position.

First though came the said draw in early December, which of course would have added significance to any prospective new manager if the lottery produced plum top seed teams in Italy, Holland or England.

As mentioned, World Cup draws where the likes of North Korea, Palestine and Dutch Antilles have the briefest place in the spotlight are convoluted affairs, but obviously the main attention circles around UEFA's teams. South America's giants do not take part in the draw, as the federation's qualifying series simply involves all ten nations playing each other home and away over three years.

The Friday night draw was to place European teams into eight groups, with the lowest seeded teams drawn first. Northern Ireland were fifth seeds and followed Azerbaijan into Group 6. Theoretically the rest of the teams could have been Scotland (third) Wales (fourth) Republic of Ireland (second) and England (first). It was not far off, as Wales and latterly England was drawn, giving an interviewed Jim Boyce the widest grin in memory. Not surprising, as Windsor Park would be sold out, advertising and sponsorship revenue would pour in and Northern Ireland would gain massive media exposure. Also a new manager would get to grapple with Beckham, Owen and Erikkson. However, media income from television rights would not boom as the IFA had an insured agreement with telecasters, guaranteeing an income whomsoever Northern Ireland would draw.

Early 2004 naturally saw speculation rising as to who would get the top job, with Jimmy Nicholl, Billy Bingham's number two, being the favourite and Lawrie Sanchez an outsider, as the selection panel whittled the candidates down to two. Sanchez played three times for Northern Ireland in the late eighties, but was more famously known for scoring 'crazy gang' Wimbledon's winning goal in the 1988 Cup Final and leading unfancied Wycombe to an FA Cup semi final. When Nicholl apparently disputed the managerial post over money, the IFA turned to Sanchez, which was no bad thing in my opinion as a manager was in the offing to whom money may not have been everything. It seemed he wanted to genuinely turnaround a team whose fortunes had reached genuine crisis proportions: shorn of confidence and simply unable to score.

Sanchez brought some of his ex- Wimbledon 'gang' with him, as a backroom team and included David Beasant, he of Cup Final penalty save fame, and Terry Gibson. Also on board was Gerry Armstrong, of Spain '82 fame, who had been assistant to Bryan Hamilton in the late 90's.

Unsurprisingly, Sanchez saw the need to get a squad nucleus together and quickly, with David Currie's office, arranged a host of spring friendlies, culminating in the proposed Caribbean tour.

Norway were first up on the February friendly date and came to Windsor Park, which was not surprisingly sold out, stressing Lesley and other front house staff, as I witnessed many personal queries and phone calls being dealt with great aplomb.

I was, and still am quite bemused, by the public who cannot accept the negative answer. One lady came in the office, looking for Family Enclosure tickets. Lesley responded by saying they were sold, to which a 'Why?' came back and a further '...but I only want four' response occurred. She would not take the fact the area was sold out and huffed her way out of the office: a scenario similar to when entry was denied to trouble causing students at the Student Union. At least Lesley was not threatened with discrimination law, mobs, knives and the like, but I know how she felt.

The atmosphere in Vaughan's (formerly Hunter's) and inside the ground seemed genuinely optimistic: like a new term at school, with its polished floor and newly whitewashed, non-graffited, walls.

Unfortunately the optimism soon turned to gloom and cries of 'Same old..same old' as Northern Ireland were 0-3 down at half time, looking nervous at the back and lacklustre in the few created attacks. I do not consider myself a football pundit in any way, shape, or form, but more a guy who likes international football, travel and a laugh. However, from my perch, and I have chimed on about this through various managerial reigns, I believe Northern Ireland's problems in attack lie with the style of play, with the team only rarely seeming to get men in front of the ball. Statistically this can be seen by how many times the offside flag is, or was, raised in a game. It's rarely, if ever, and perhaps little wonder it took two years to score a goal since the Poland game in Limassol.

It did come though, early in the second half courtesy of David Healy. Talk about party, Northern Ireland's supporters went crazy; missing the fact Norway restored their three goal lead within a minute. It did not matter; the hoo-do was broken after 1296 minutes, with the Spion Stand breaking into a 'conga'. Lawrie Sanchez had suggested in his programme notes that his prerogative in the game was most likely to score against, rather than beat, the Norwegians, which was done though apparently the 2 year goal drought represented the longest period in UEFA history, that an affiliate had gone without scoring. Longer than 'basket' cases, including San Marino, Liechtenstein and the Faeroes.

The press produced the most positive spin on a 1-4 defeat imaginable, and there did seem genuine hope that Sanchez' charges could at least become competitive. Roll on Estonia!

ESTONIA REVISITED

In purely financial terms, the trip to Estonia came a few months early, because in early May the country joined the EU talking shop. The country had evolved from an ex-Soviet republic in 1991 to an independent 'friendly' nation within 13 years; no mean achievement, but in March 2004 the budget airlines had not yet incorporated capital Tallinn into their routes, as the accession was not complete. Hence a £250+ airfare via Finnair had to be paid for a two day trip.

Personally, I take some trips, such as a visit to Spain or Italy as a footballing necessity, but I was really looking forward to a return to Estonia. I say return, because I had been to Tallinn in summer 1995, to find some relief from a British heat wave and a tosser of a line manager.

I do not do 'hot' and felt a real necessity to escape in 1995, just to cool down. The people who arranged my trip to Riga in early 1995 were specialists in the (slowly) emerging Eastern Europe and offered a great deal on a three-city Baltic tour, taking in 'cooler' Helsinki, Tallinn and Vilnius. Also I could 'chill' from the incessant bullying dished out by an insecure regional manager.

I am not prepared to name this guy or the company involved, but I often wonder how guys like this get senior positions. He could not understand why my business was struggling, despite the site being 60% surrounded by sand and sea and being at the mercy of a heat wave. Put it this way, if you were on a family holiday in Bexhill, would you want to entertain your kids in a non-air conditioned tin hut, complete with 26 heat creating motors, or supervising them on a sun drenched picnic laden beach?

My manager was convinced the former should predominate and often swore at, bullied and harangued members of staff, as results did not (obviously) match expectations.

I can put up with constructive working criticism, but will never accept humiliation and I clearly made my feelings felt, to which his bitterness became more acute as he was spoken to by personnel officers. As such, I needed to escape the 'kitchen' and take the trip to the Baltic.

1995 Tallinn was struggling. It had badly fractured infrastructure, with poorly maintained roads and ramshackle trams and Trabants aplenty. (A Trabant was the East German 'peoples' car, of which little else positive can be said, save they had four wheels, a chassis and an engine and mostly got those fortunate to own one from A to B.)

The previously mentioned 'rotten' smell was prominent, particularly as the British heat wave was almost as acute in Estonia, and Russian prostitutes were literally everywhere. They are impossible to miss given their 'uniform' comprising the shortest skirts imaginable, harsh facial make-up and, of course, 'kinky boots'. Not taking this avenue of entertainment, I took the option of watching a Baltic Cup encounter between Estonia and Lithuania, which finished 0-1 to the visitors.

Fast forward 9 years and it was like comparing black against white. Volvo and Mercedes taxis aplenty, plate glass offices, class hotels, a restored 'café-style' old-town, complete with tourist shops, and no prostitutes in every hotel lobby. Congratulations to Tallinn and Estonia, no doubt aided by neighbouring Finland and the EU, for changing their society to one which actually felt welcoming, down to the redeveloped Scandic Palace Hotel, booked courtesy of Rebecca.

It was just a little cold though, with Robert having to alter his travel plans across the Baltic from Helsinki to air from boat as the port was still frozen from the winter's harshness. There was certainly no power in the late winter sunshine, coupled to the biting East wind, as me and Robert assessed respective Flora Tallinn pitches where both internationals were to be played. I say both, because Jim had arranged a supporter's match, which took place on an astro-turf pitch in the Flora complex.

It was a lunchtime kick-off; arranged after a group of supporters had visited the place where Ulster's Joey Dunlop met his death.

Dunlop was perhaps the world's best and most well known road race motorcycling star, often winning the Isle of Man TT races and feted at Ulster's 'NorthWest' 200 motorcycling festival. This takes place in mid-May and is the most watched sports event in Europe, behind the Tour de France. However, Dunlop became a posthumous legend in 2004, as he was killed racing in Estonia, where road racing, unlike most of mainland Europe and the UK was not banned. Northern Ireland supporters felt they needed to pay their respects, before losing 3-4 to the Estonians in a rather messy affair, no doubt hindered by the previous nights drinks, which came in at around 50p per half litre of beer.

As for the full international, some sixty hardy souls were on parade looking for Sanchez to 'improve' on the goal against Norway. Sure enough, a David Healy thunderbolt separated the two teams as Northern Ireland WON, yes WON, 1-0. Unfortunately for some, including Alan Ferris and 'Scouse' Andy, the goal came in the 44th minute. This is often seen as the best time for a team to score, for various psychological reasons, but it is a supporter's nightmare.

Usually football grounds have a clock which can count down from 45(minutes) to zero, but a more sure-fire sign that half time is coming up, is the fourth official showing off an illuminated board with the amount of extra-time which has to be played. This though can be a cue for supporters to make an early run for the pie stall, or more likely the toilet before you get stuck in a queue of a hundred to piss, behind a bloke who has decided to read the match programme in the sit down cubicle. Numerous of the travelling legion decided the option of lager relief could not wait and missed the said piece of history.

They did not miss that other match day regular though: the over zealous match day steward (or ****in' dickhead), whom I feel deserves a mention in reference to this game. We all know the type: the steward who craves authority, by checking every ticket at every opportunity, by making sure everyone sits in the correct seat and gets the law involved the slightest moment he feels his miniscule control is under threat. My father, when we went to golf events used to say, 'Give 'em an armband and they think they're God!', as they decided when and where the watching public went. The person in question in Estonia saw fit to spend the game bursting the green balloons we had let drift in the wind with a pin as they fell to the floor. Hardly diverting possible crowd disorder, but something constructive to tell the wife!

In conclusion, as far as the football was concerned, Sanchez' new Northern Ireland had successfully completed the second mission, in beating a team placed some forty places above them in the world rankings.

The next step was in late April to test their competitiveness against a top European team, as Serbia & Montenegro, formerly Yugoslavia, visited Windsor Park.

EYES FACING WEST

Northern Ireland had played what was then known as Yugoslavia (but was only the states of Serbia and Montenegro as Bosnia, Slovenia, Croatia and Macedonia had become autonomous entities) in summer 2000 and the poignancy of such a fixture has already been mentioned, as the Yugoslavs visited Belfast in 1975, when nobody else wanted to. The match programme was informative in this respect, but also saw fit to mention other 'positive' statistics, such as the monkey of the goal scoring drought was off the team's back; Northern Ireland not having won a home friendly for six years (a fact which still existed a year later) or going up nine places to 115 in the world rankings.

On the pitch, there were many positive vibes as the team deservedly held the Serbs 1-1, and amongst the faithful there was genuine optimism that, whilst not being world beaters, the team could be a match for most middle ranking European teams, such as Hungary, Switzerland, Slovenia and the like. It appeared Sanchez was playing to the strengths he had, with Mark Williams and Aaron Hughes marshalling the defence and a combative midfield including Keith Gillespie and Tommy Docherty.

However, as far as I was concerned, I was in blatant holiday mode, as people were asking what my/our plans were for the Caribbean tour.

They could have asked in January, as this was when Robert (with his wife) and I took a punt on the itinerary and booked a 12 day trip to the West Indies. Rebecca did not want to come, as she had no interest in suffering the tropical humidity in the likes of Trinidad.

In Estonia, I had taken a large Denmark flag, which I had 'borrowed' from a Calais council flagpole, emblazoned with the message 'Ban Jamaica'. This was because Jamaica had unilaterally pulled out of the opening fixture on the tour, choosing instead to play a three team tournament including the Republic, and threw our travel plans into disarray. Hurriedly on the announcement Barbados had stepped into the breach, I went to Thomas Cook in Luton and booked some return transfers between Jamaica and Barbados.

Once completed, the total flight bill per person for the trip, which included most island hops was £1225 each.

The emphasis is on 'most' here, because the January punt gambled on the Trinidad & Tobago game being on the major island. It wasn't, being staged in the Dwight Yorke stadium in Tobago, meaning another flight had to be booked. I suffered the financial 'hit' though as the cost of the 18 minute flight was £54 for the three of us.

By late March therefore it was a wrap, with eight flights booked and hotels reserved and everything crossed for the last weekend in May. My final thought was Liat and British West Indian Airways MUST run to time, as island hopping was a must.

CARIBBEAN REALITY

Travel Agents are like insurance agents, in that they are great at taking your money, as the full fares for the Caribbean had to be paid up front in January. However, when the Jamaica leg was replaced by a Barbados stopover, Thomas Cook would not change the itinerary, which just could be acceptable, but the way the barriers were put up was most annoying. But no bother, the three of us were in this and had to take the risks; the main one being that our extra flight via Barbados, which was an in and out job so as to hook up with our already booked flights, only had a forty minute turnaround.

As for the hotels, the internet was the main avenue of communication and very much in the lap of website photographs.

Robert and me were also somewhat concerned that there were three on the trip, but need not have been as Yvonne was a great traveller, though she was always prodding the male folk, due to our notorious snoring!

She did not do this on the outward flight to Kingston in Jamaica though, as a plane profile cock-up led us to having a British Airways upgrade to club class. Things do not get much better than this, as I had experienced an upgrade on a return flight from New York in January, all because of FIFA.

Jason Aspinall is a neighbour of publican Keith in North Wales, and though we did not know each other, we grew up in the same town, Lytham. He was now a flight steward for BA and I asked him if there was any chance of an upgrade on mine and Rebecca's surprise weekend trip to New York. He tried his best and suggested we turned up booted and suited just in case. I was like a fish out of water in economy class and felt distinctly uncomfortable amongst the 'Essex family' types going on a jolly.

Arrival in the States can obviously be an time consuming affair, as the Americans try to deny entry to undesirables. Hence a large queue formed and a member of the BA ground grew noted I was wearing a FIFA lapel badge on my jacket. Alfredo asked if I was involved in FIFA and I answered negatively, but we passed the time of day and I insisted he had the badge as he had noticed it. He was most gracious and suggested he would leave something for us at the check-in desk on our return home. He was true to his word, leaving two Club Class upgrades worth around £4,000! Champagne and smoked salmon bagels all the way home. I cannot remember where I got the badge from, but David Currie comes to mind, and in short, 'thank you very much'!

I therefore knew what I was getting on the way to Kingston, with an extended seat, champagne, and total waiter service, a great novelty for all concerned and a wonderful way to start the holiday.

Not so for Justin, his brother or Paul Duffin, as BA lost Justin's baggage, but the compensation was we were all staying in the Kingston Hilton, which Rebecca had managed to book for us three at a preferential rate courtesy of manager Nellie Ann.

We were all happy to stay in an all inclusive property, as Kingston was a frightening place. People hanging around on street corners creating a menacing atmosphere and one not conducive to a night on the town. Robert and Yvonne were even scared when they went for a walk at 6am, noting a sign suggesting marriages were banned in the local park. I never ventured that far and was glad to journey back to the airport in our commandeered camper taxi

We did stop briefly for a photo shoot against a road sign displaying Ulster Avenue and noted the beauty of the Blue Mountains, which made a spectacular backdrop.

It was a pity in retrospect Marty Lowry was not at said photo shoot, as he has an authentic road sign in his hallway of Ulster Place: a gift from the Queen Mother.

Whilst working at the International Students' House, accommodation in the form of a bed-sit was proffered, which created a great situation; living in Regent's Park for free, with Oxford Street and Piccadilly Circus the local shopping centres. Of course, there was a steady stream of visitors coming to see the sites, one of which was Marty, who took in a Charlton v Nottingham Forest match, in between being green with envy over the name of a street close to where I lived in York Terrace. It was Ulster Place, which linked to Ulster Terrace, and Marty was pondering the possibility of a road sign going missing.

Some time later I noticed said sign had been ripped from the railings and was technically available for removal. As I often worked until 4am, the Crown Estates, which were then Queen Mother owned lost said sign. It blew away in the wind, honest, to Leuchars via Easyjet and Scotrail one evening, where Marty was then living whilst working at the RAF base. This brief sojourn also included our spectating at a Cowdenbeath v Falkirk Cup match and then a flit to catch the last half hour of the East Fife v St.Mirren match. The former match was quite bizarre in that there were too many spectators and the caterers ran out of pies! Judging by their bellies, that was something numerous Americans at nearby St.Andrews were not short of, as we spent the following afternoon sitting by The Road Hole on the Old Course, which has a hostelry close by, informing the golfers how crap they were.

Returning to the Caribbean, we took a direct flight to Barbados, checking into the most idyllic beach hotel, which was literally a 15 step walk, via a swimming pool, into the Atlantic Ocean. The same Atlantic which is always grey and dirty, even in Blackpool's high summer, was now turquoise blue with warm feeling bunker coloured silky white sand slipping between my toes. I had never ever paddled in the sea before now and the feeling was incredibly therapeutic until a breaker arrived and soaked my shorts, but it made me understand why people save and save to have a holiday of a lifetime in places like this, particularly to watch cricket matches. Sure it was hot, but even I could have got used to this. Not so perhaps in the cold light of day of having to find work and battle against the devastating hurricanes which swept the region the proceeding autumn.

A Barbados Sunday was quiet, as the locals seemed quite God-fearing and church going, with capital Georgetown closed, even for a drink. On meeting other supporters at the ground, they had found an impromptu bar/club on a Georgetown beach, allowing entry by tag system, and nothing else.

Bus drivers however, were not celebrating holy Sunday, as their operation was a private one as drivers and mates drove on routes on crew buses, pipping at and waving down prospective customers. Of course, we took to this mode of transport, enjoying the decibel pounding reggae music and German tourists on our knees as the seats were crammed. So loud was the music that the mode of communication was a bang on the roof, but the most surreal experience was two number 11 drivers arguing for our custom at shed/shack central bus station.

At the National Stadium, the atmosphere amongst the supporters was most cordial as the 30 odd supporters were all exchanging notes on how they travelled, how long they were staying for and where they were going next. Everyone seemed to know each other, but it seemed numerous had had to holiday in Jamaica, as they booked and paid in the spring and could then only take in one fixture due to the expense. Thanks Jamaica.

The match was played at little more than walking pace, as the Northern Ireland players were clearly suffering from climate change and jet lag, having only arrived some 24hours previously. The final score was 1-1 and was ruined by an plainly incompetent referee, who was quite clearly a 'homer' and greatly annoyed a seething Lawrie Sanchez and his back room team, of which David Beasant took a supporters' ribbing with a ringing chant of 'Salad Cream'. This humour came about because in 1992 Beasant had to withdraw from the England squad, prior to European finals, as he injured his toe by dropping a bottle of salad cream on it.

Press, players and supporters all met up the following morning at the airport as most went their separate ways onwards to St.Kitts. We went, with a photographed Curtley Ambrose, the scourge of England's batsmen in the 1990's, to Antigua, with the help of a BWIA stewardess, who willingly cut a return flight to Jamaica out of our schedule.

DEAD BORED IN ST. JOHN'S

This book has a few travel tips in it, but one piece of serious advice is never to visit Antigua on Whit Monday. Capital St. John's was closed, save for a Kentucky Fried Chicken and a late night general store. Robert was sick and I amused myself watching West Indies play Bangladesh and baseball on New York's CBS station. There were no tourist shops and not even a place to eat or get an ice cream. The boredom ultimately became so acute that we spent half an hour on a moored boat looking around a religious book fayre! Tuesday could not arrive quick enough as we moved on to St.Kitts.

For me, this was by far the most pleasant and enjoyable island we visited as it was the most laid back and traditional. Cane growing in the fields, no sense of fear on the streets, and people just wandering around doing their business without honking taxis and street corner gangs. One group of workers were tending the roadside as we passed by on the way to the hotel, yet when I walked to capital Basseterre, all the road crew were having siestas in hammocks! As an aside, the trip to the hotel in York's camper van was via Kim Collins Avenue, the Kim Collins roundabout and most probably Kim Collins everywhere else, for Collins was the then world 100 metres athletics champion.

The Beach Cove Hotel was a complex overlooking the Basseterre bay and one that we shared with the official party, mostly in the swimming pool, as it was simply somewhere to keep cool. It was also somewhere I learnt how to swim!

I don't do swimming as I have a sight problem and shimmering water in Lytham swimming baths freaked me out as an eight year old. Necessity in 1989 meant I had to learn to swim a little, but it was no more than scrabbling my way across a hotel pool. However, the IFA's temporary team doctor offered her advice on getting higher in the water and it simply did the trick. I would not go in the sea though like the doctor, who scuba'd around the bay, swimming numerous miles.

Robert and Yvonne wanted to chill on this sun drenched afternoon and mindful that they needed their space I wandered off to the capital.

The main street had open drains and chickens roaming around, but also carried a massive banner spanning its width suggesting, 'The Big Clash…The Biggest Ever', and advertising the St.Kitts v Northern Ireland match.

Most would think a Brazil v Argentina or an England v Scotland match up was big but not this big, with the game at the national stadium; the same stadium which 27 hours before the big match kicked off was being mown by a flock of goats. The pitch had two open sides, one literally neighbouring the cricket square an old style 'scratching' shed and an antiquated concrete grandstand. This housed the St.Kitt's and St. Nevis FA and I entered the office looking for a poster, to which a secretary said 'Tell your boys we're altering the time of the fixture to 8.00(pm) so you will have a better chance of beating us'.

With a St.Kitts v USA, 'Biggest game ever…' (!) poster, I took this information back to the hotel and told the crowd around the swimming pool to which David Currie suggested was a wind up. It wasn't, but was important to David, who would have to inform the manager and re-arrange eating times, particularly on the afternoon of the match. This would not be too easy as the catering was very much a 'you eat when we are here', school dinner type operation, rather than a customer led affair, unlike the bar which thankfully was always available. Even after the match, numerous supporters and press returned to the hotel to find no food available. Now I am not a magician, but I did manage to make numerous sandwiches from a baguette and some plastic cheese, but believe me the bread was mighty thin!

Match night, complete with face paint and a Northern Ireland Hawaiian strip, bordered between surreal and farcical. The goats had gone, but the pitch was barely marked, no perimeter had been defined, and the spectacle was ruined given the howling gale which blew across the pitch.

The records show Northern Ireland won this game 2-0, but the performance was poor, with two late goals only breaking the deadlock. It was a disjointed display, featuring a spectacular Paul McVeigh miss, and typified a squad performance. Though a rarity for Northern Ireland to take on a tour like this, England, and more pertinently, rugby teams often tour, and ensure everyone at least gets a run out. This was the way the management team looked on this, playing fringe players until the last half hour, when the likes of Gillespie and Healy joined the fray to attempt to secure a result. A late night chat with David Beasant confirmed this scenario, in that everyone needed to play, but ultimately a result was needed, as well as the 'first' team needing to fully prepare for what was the more serious match against Trinidad and Tobago at the weekend.

We left St.Kitt's at lunchtime the following day, for the next leg, destination Port of Spain, having missed the mass populace of monkeys in the St.Kitt's mountains, but attempting to remedy things in a Trinidad swamp.

The capital of T&T is perhaps akin to somewhere like Wolverhampton, very functional with oppressive humidity, but there was no beach and once a tour of the shops had been done, there was little else to savour, save watching the world go by on the bizarre Savanna Park. This area is also known as the biggest roundabout in the world, and is grassland, easily the size of Regents Park on which youngsters seemed to play their games. Robert therefore decided we should do something touristy and it was agreed we would part with US$20 each and take on a wildlife tour of the local swampland. Bored was not the answer for this, as a three hour boat trip yielded two sleeping tree snakes and a couple of flocks of flamingos in between the tropical showers. I quickly turned my attention to taking the piss out of three Chinese tourists at the front of the boat, who were on a junket from their Embassy, complete with their three cameras; cine, digital and pocket!

I often wonder what an Oriental holiday snap evening is like, concluding they must be popular given that those of that race always have piles of the latest camera equipment weighing off their necks.

Match day Sunday meant using our £18 plane tickets and hopping over to Tobago for an afternoon out at the Dwight Yorke Stadium, set in the Tobago rainforest.

Tobago was shut, as is usual on a 'religious' Sunday, save for Kentucky Fried Chicken, meaning we were at the ground four hours prior to kick off. We quickly discovered though whilst in transit is that one industry which seemed to flourish on both islands, regardless of the day was taxiing (tourists).

At the airport numerous people wanted to offer their cars, both officially and on a more freelance basis. One such was a lady who offered a trip to and from the ground: a grateful service for the return as the melee outside the ground after the game was particularly acute. A similar unofficial taxi scenario was apparent on the journey back to the hotel on return to Tobago, with a car that had broken window handles, Robert holding the door closed and me observing the driver holding the electrics together as he drove along. I suppose a $20 one off fair for hanging around the airport could be a worthwhile occupation if a local didn't fancy watching television!

At the game, both a bizarre incident occurred and history was made.

Bizarreness came in the form of Dwight Yorke, who was wooed from the stands to play the second half for the home team. Yorke was a class striker, who played, and scored vital goals for Manchester United, whilst at their zenith in the late 90s, but was a fading light once his ego got the better of him and was seen as surplus stock at Old Trafford. In this game though, he tried to take on a role of sweeper/midfield play maker, a la Dunga or Socrates from great Brazilian teams and made a total pratt of himself. His fitness was poor and skill totally lacking for this role. No bother, as it helped Northern Ireland win 3-0.

Two of the goals, the first of which was a 40 yard chip shot over an arguing home team goalkeeper came from David Healy. His second was history making as he became Northern Ireland's highest scorer, overtaking the Clarke/Gillespie mark of thirteen. I have seen every one of Healy's goals and apart from penalties, they are usually pretty spectacular, as I recollect his drives against Denmark and Estonia, the mentioned Trinidad chip and later goals against Wales and Austria in 2004. I congratulate Healy's efforts because he toiled long and hard, in the barren years of 2002 and 2003, never giving up and often chasing lost, nigh hopeless, causes. I regularly wear his Greece shirt with pride, as do his family, often seen at Windsor Park wearing green no.9 tops.

GROUCHED IN PARADISE

As far as I am concerned, when a match is over, the trip or holiday is over. However, it's not too easy to travel back home on the first BA shuttle from Port of Spain, as if it were Zurich or Tallinn and be in the office for 9 am. Our journey home involved another trip to Antigua to hook up with a BA jumbo for an overnight (on Tuesday) flight back to Heathrow. This was the most tiresome part of the trip. There was nothing to look forward to any more. No matches, and no new sites, just St.John's for a day and a couple of airport waits. Even the photo call at the cricket ground where Brian Lara had piled up 400 runs against England in March seemed boring. Time was dragging, there seemed nothing to talk about, even the ice cream tasted bland and I spent most of the Tuesday afternoon on the internet asking whether religious fanatics were hypocrites! With hindsight I realised I had never been away from home for so long, as I do not do two weeks on the beach in Malaga and had not noticed that I was fed up with carrying my bag around, packing and unpacking, and sitting in sweaty pants. I just wanted my own bed and pillow. I hope Robert and Yvonne had not noticed either!

I was delighted therefore when we got our taxi to VC Bird airport. However, on arrival I got the feeling something was not right. There were too many people standing around with similarly large suitcases, looking frustrated and forlorn. Somehow, we managed to check-in, get a seat reservation and get our bags tagged and taken, but were told NOT to go through customs. Slightly confused, we saw a BA captain and asked what was going on. He thought he had a problem with the plane, but was assuring and told us to listen out for more information.

We did and were told we were being shipped off to a hotel for the night as the plane was in pieces: literally.

The hotel was an all inclusive idyllic affair, with free food, bars and synthetic beaches to soak up the sun. Wedding parties were enjoying themselves, but we wanted to go home, particularly as I saw the normal guests going about their business. It was akin to pigs in a trough, as they swilled as much alcohol as they could at the bar, and ate as much as they could at feeding time. At breakfast, groups sat and three hours later the same groups sat, doing the same thing. It was simply sad. Many of these people would see this holiday as heaven, and recount their trip to Antigua, but it isn't that. It is transportation into a mock paradise and holiday makers love it as they are free from freedom and all the hazards it brings. No need to cook, moreover to think and worry. Yet within a mile of the gates are the peasant cane and pineapple growers. Surely that is Antigua, not as much food and drink as your stomach can, or cannot, bear. Safe to say I would put all inclusive holidays into Room 101! I even refused to take a photo of the beach, as I did not consider myself on holiday anymore. I was angry and wanted to be home and whether true or not, am still convinced BA stalled the flight to get a full plane load of people on board the day after, to save money.

It certainly didn't save Robert and Yvonne money, as they had to buy new flights back to Belfast at a cost of £200, despite BA assurances in Antigua. As I have mentioned before, airlines and insurance companies are great until there is a problem! Thomas Cook refused to pay out, as the insurance ended when the Tuesday flight left. It didn't though; the moral of the tale being to read the small print! On a brighter personal note though, as that flight left St.John's I quietly celebrated 9 years of watching every Northern Ireland game. This trip had been the biggest challenge time wise, and the flexibility of BWIA helped towards that, particularly in cutting out the Jamaica return trip. Another unsuspecting patron to the cause!

DOES IT MATTER ANYMORE?

The time, 18.30, on a balmy summer Friday evening: the place The Grovefield Hotel, Maidenhead: the date Friday 7th July. Funny how you always remember shattering or infamous dates for various reasons, but this was scary.

I occasionally do some 'mystery' shop work for various companies, which means buying something in a shop or restaurant, gauging the service and seeing what the produce tastes like. Sometimes this meant eating motorway service food, which is akin to swallowing last Friday night's regurgitated kebab, or occasionally spending the night in a flash hotel or serviced apartment, eating gastro-grub and basically being on a jolly.

Rebecca and me were doing the latter and whilst showering I noticed a lump in my testicles. Yes, I did drop the soap and started frantically inspecting my family allowance, which was not the most satisfying experience anyway as I had a testicular torsion from playing rugby some years previously. In a few instants I can desperately remember poking around hoping it was a myth, but to no avail and on informing Rebecca was on her phone to the doctor in seconds, who was personally reassuring and booked an appointment within four days. However, it doesn't stop your own personal rumour mill going into overdrive and save to say dinner did not taste so good and the crisp hotel bed sheets ended up as being decidedly clammy as I spent the night tossing (!), turning and sweating profusely.

Those four days were spent soul searching and comfort eating, and in this whole experience I gained a stone in weight until its successful conclusion on a damp

November Friday at Luton and Dunstable hospital. It wasn't reassuring when I met the doctor who said 'I don't think its cancer, but we had better get it checked'. The word had been mentioned. Suddenly things like getting pissed in the summer sunshine at Lord's, or even watching Northern Ireland, weren't important anymore. Sure that may sound like a cliché, but now self-preservation was all encompassing.

Football wise though, Northern Ireland had arranged a friendly for mid-August against Switzerland and I did consider not going, but then thought if this thing was bad, I might not get to too many more games. Therefore, I booked a flight to Zurich and booked a day's holiday, just going to and from the game overnight.

My new employers, Remarkable Restaurants had only two office staff; one of which is Liz Pallace, a (semi) football widow to a Newcastle United husband and family, who saw my blue dot go on the wall calendar to signify a day off. She asked out of interest what was going on and I explained myself, to which she replied by saying 'Oh! I thought it would be something silly like that'. I understood the word 'silly' had a touch of sarcasm, but this was coming from the accountant, who has to be at the helm of the maddest company I have ever been involved with. It is run (hands-off) by an eccentric ex-Olympic swimmer called Robert Thomas, (and his wife Jean) who changed the name of one of his pubs to The Swimmer at the Grafton Arms from the simple Grafton Arms and adorned it with swimming medals. He once ran a business selling Routemaster buses to the States and has some joint pub partnerships with an ageing hippy in Julian, who was once the lodger to Robert and his girlfriend Cecilia, who is now Julian's wife! Hence things can get a bit hot when those holding the playing cards (pubs) fall out, which is alarmingly regular, if and when they are on speaking terms. So my doing something silly like a day trip to Switzerland was probably par for the course.

Due to my ongoing scare though, it was not a happy trip, as Robert would concur. He could see something was wrong, as did Leslie and Paul in Belfast three weeks later.

I told Rebecca I would suffer any ramifications from this lump in silence and tell nobody, as I was not looking for a sympathy vote or people asking how I was. I did tell Robert though I may have a problem and was astounded to hear Corney (Portadown Gareth) was undergoing chemotherapy and naturally requested my wishes be passed on.

I had also been to Zurich three times before and consider it functional rather than fun, with the avenues of designer shops emphasising the cities' accompanying opulence, rather than the bars and brothels of say, Amsterdam or Dortmund. When making a repeat city visit, I also find it bizarre that I remember tiny things, like for example, knowing the number 4 tram takes you to the Grasshopper Stadium from the central station!

This was the same stadium which was synonymous with Bryan Hamilton's demise in 1997, but this time things were different on two counts. Northern Ireland firstly gave an assured rather than a disastrous performance, and deserved a 0-0 draw, with the defence holding up particularly well. Second, there were 100 supporters in situ, rather than one; all of whom were 'regulars'. I define regulars as faces you may know to say hello to at a match, but know little more about them than they watch Northern Ireland. Paul Duffin, (Scouse) Andy, Stuarty Mc-, Mad Dog 'Neil', Skin and Winston, Jim Rainey and 'Silver' Ferris turn up at most or all games, and then go home again, not to be seen until the next time; with their own personal tales of supporters games, lap dancing clubs, with or without local television personalities, and drunken pranks in rooftop swimming pools. From a personal point of view, I would like to spend more time with some supporters on away jaunts, but going to every game means taking a lot of time off and if I only take a day off, then it (unfortunately) helps with company holidays.

However, there is one thing I can never understand with some supporters and that is the drink scenario.

I like a drink as much as the next bloke, but I also like to remember most of my match experience, good bad or otherwise, rather than fall asleep for the game due to the local juices. It is similar to Christmas and New Year revellers, whom I would like to ask what they remembered about their celebration. Having said that, it never ceases to amaze me when I see the resourcefulness of supporters in their attempt to get cheap booze. In Zurich, they found out that wine in the supermarket was cheaper than beer, at CHF 3 a bottle, whilst in Iceland numerous joined a student union type operation to get around the extortionate on sales prices, which started at around £4 a half litre.

It appeared therefore the team were heading into the World Cup qualifying campaign in a positive frame of mind, buoyed up by a six match unbeaten run, and knowledge the home games would be played in front of sold-out audiences. With England, and to a lesser extent Wales, visiting Windsor Park, demand for 'season' tickets far outstripped the 11,000 odd capacity.

The first game of the series was Northern Ireland's first home Saturday fixture since Denmark in 2000, against an unpredictable Poland side, in early September.

Poland are one of international football's great enigmas, flattering to deceive on occasions like the 2002 World Cup qualification, when they stormed through a group with ease and were then a flop in the Far East, despite being seen as a dark horse by many. Also there were the tales from the 70's and early 90's, when Poland stood in the way, successfully in the former, of England's interest in final competitions. For the present though, Poland were second seeds in this group, and probably the weakest on paper, at that, bearing in mind Denmark, Turkey and Ukraine were also in the second seeds pot the previous December in Germany.

Personally, I was very hopeful that this could, just could, be Northern Ireland's chance to make an impression on a qualifying series, though no bookmaker was willing to take my £5 on Northern Ireland finishing second in the group.

Unfortunately the pre-game optimism lasted three minutes, when a communication mix-up in politically correct talk, saw a Polish corner enter the Northern Ireland net. Two further goals put the fixture beyond doubt, leaving what can only be described as amazing support very deflated. Simply everywhere on the Lisburn Road was green, prior to the game as late summer sunshine allowed for a (match) shirt sleeve day and Vaughan's, who do not endear themselves to match day supporters, despite being the nearest hostelry to Windsor Park, was full and raucous soon after twelve, some three hours before kick-off.

Some of the Belfast green-ness is due to successful supporters clubs, Marty's on-line fanzine, and a community relations drive by the IFA, led by Michael Boyd, but today was a great occasion and on such rarities, I just wished the English press who derided Northern Ireland in my former years as a 'Dodge City' and latterly, and correctly, over the Neil Lennon affair, could report the facts from today. They would hopefully, get a chance a few days later when the now christened 'Green and White Army' visited Cardiff to play Wales.

AWAY AT HOME AND AWAY AWAY, IF YOU SEE WHAT I MEAN

As a company auditor, I can make statistics read anything as can politicians for that fact. For example, in 1980s recession savaged Britain I remember Mrs. Thatcher suggesting it was commendable that well over 85% of Britons of working age were in employment. It sounds good, given the high number, but what about the other 15% struggling on state benefits!

Not dissimilar statistics came out for the Wales game in that more supporters were 'travelling' to this game, than heads had attended friendlies at Windsor Park. In 1996 only 3,500 had been present at friendlies against Norway and Sweden and even in 2000 the attendance for the Yugoslavia game was only 6,600. Of course, since then Northern Ireland's support had been galvanised, but it was bizarre that for the 'home' international fixtures in England and Wales, there was likely to be more 'away' support than there had been home support.

This is a quirk caused by the UK having four national teams, but surely it adds weight to Jim Boyce's argument for a return of the Home International Championship. It's unlikely to happen, given the English FA's intransigence and need to play friendlies against advertising friendly opposition such as Japan and Saudi Arabia, but hope springs eternal as they say. Personally, I hope one day the English FA do need to resurrect this once great end of season competition and Jim Boyce et al tell them to go and play South Korea to put it nicely.

The game against Wales was a 'home' game for me in that these legions of supporters were to all intents and purposes visiting my island: all 5,000 of them. Gavin

(Lavery) and Ian flew into Luton and the car took us to Cardiff, though such was the beauty of the day, that Gavin suggested we '***k the football and went to the (Whipsnade) Zoo!'. No chance, as this was a game I had waited a long time for. A competitive local derby, the first for a generation.

On arrival at Cardiff, green and white again was everywhere and the Welsh, in particular the traders, were broadly welcoming. That's not surprising. 5,000 supporters made the trip, all needing to be fed and watered to varying degrees: a pure licence to print money, as the managers of places like The Walkabout would testify. Several hundred supporters all on the drink, all behaving themselves and filling the tills. Manna from heaven in midweek.

This is the reason why you never hear of publicans abroad complaining when the likes of England are in town. Yes, the police and riot squads may have to clean up the mess, but a publican would likely take a punt that his retirement plan will boom over a match day trip, simply because of the amount of lager he will sell to British tourists. He works on the idea that he pays his insurance against his pub getting wrecked, but the insurance don't pay out if he closes down. Therefore British football supporters equate to dollar signs rather than the French who go for the social experience or maybe the Turks, who fanatically support their team, but do little else, unless the British hooligan element is in town.

I didn't contribute to the Welsh economy, save for a few bottles of mineral water, because I was on driving duty. I was quite happy with that scenario, as I could remember most of the game and its build up, without it being clouded in alcoholic haze. The game was a magnificent affair, but could have been a whole lot better, with Northern Ireland 2-0 ahead after 15 minutes. The atmosphere was initially electric, but then became somewhat subdued after the second goal as the Italian referee lost his senses and red-carded David Healy, for supposedly gesturing to the crowd, only minutes after sending off Michael Hughes and Wales' Robbie Savage for a 'local derby' type tangle. As my father often said at rugby matches, 'You can have two crap sides, but not a crap ref!', and the man in black destroyed this game by his early decisions. With at least ten versus ten, Northern Ireland would have surely won the game, against a rapidly declining Wales, who seemed to be riddled with in-fighting, exposed to the public with the retirements that followed after manager Mark Hughes left to manage Blackburn. However, no matter how poor the referee was, he was the sole arbiter of fact and his personnel decision, as well as denying Northern Ireland a blatant penalty, meant Wales could get back into the game, eventually drawing 2-2.

However, the Northern Ireland supporters won their battle against 58,000 Wales supporters in the magnificent Millennium Stadium, often out cheering their hosts. There are not many groups of mass supporters who can say that! Personally, I stood by the Carrickfergus Silver Band crew, complete with the trombone playing 'Pancake', so named after being born on a 'Pancake Day' (which one?). He and other members of the band serenaded the support, to such an extent, that they ran out of 'puff' by half time. A pity that really, because the second half was like 'The Longest Night', with Northern Ireland 2-1 ahead, and trying to hold on. The rest, they say is history!

I would have loved to be part of the after-game party, but the car needed to be home with me for work! Perhaps I could celebrate a night out at the next away fixture; that being a small trip to sample the delights of Azerbaijan.

For the uninitiated, this former Soviet outpost, neighbours, and has fought wars with, Armenia and Iran. Continuing the geographical theme, the country hogs the Caspian Sea, famous for sturgeon caviar and the flight time takes longer than that to Baghdad. Also it is technically rich; oil rich that is, which was quite handy as Robert had a friend of a friend who worked there and was willing to put us up for the two nights. That was a blessing in disguise, because reports came back that the main hotel was insect infested and numerous supporters were heavily covered with mosquito bites.

A brief visit to the hotel showed it to be the spitting image of the one in Moldova: supposedly big and palatial, but very drab in communist grey concrete with most of the interior lights in public areas out of order to preserve electricity.

Azerbaijan was similar to other ex-Soviet republics in another respect, in that the authorities see the Western visitor as a bureaucratic cash cow. Naturally, this starts with visas. Moldova $80, Romania (1999) £33, Armenia on departure $20, visa $40, Ukraine $60. On this occasion, at midnight in Baku it was $46, not forgetting a $10 fee for a passport photo, just in case you didn't have one. I suppose the saving grace, apart from the local cabbies, who will try to rip you off (well it's the same in London) is the places are cheap with a low cost of living. In the dead of night, Drew had arranged a cab to his apartment, so it wasn't until daylight, or Islamic prayer time, that you could view your surroundings. Yes, 5.30 a.m. and after eight hours travelling and three hours time difference and little comfortable sleep, an Imam is calling his faithful to Allah! Not as you would notice on streets though, as this 93% Islamic state had not one veil amongst the female populace. Indeed Harrigay's Green Lanes is more an Islamic operation than Baku, where the females for example are very Russified, wearing the minimum clothing possible plus obligatory red lipstick and designer sunglasses.

Unsurprisingly, the Baku skyline was akin to Chisnau and Yerevan, with hideous down trodden tower blocks, scattered with occasional satellite dishes placed on rooftops or balconies. Drew latterly explained that inside the blocks there are more Western trappings, with those owned by the many oil interested companies having Jacuzzis, saunas and air conditioning, which is taken as a sign in Azerbaijan that one has made it! Summers in Baku have temperatures around 40 degrees for weeks on end and on their visit, Wales took many bags of cooling ice to control body heat.

The temperature in early October was far more temperate, but on the visit downtown, it was easy to see that Baku was a typical 'have and have not' economy. There were the black Mercedes and opulent Gucci type shops coupled to the half built apartment blocks, caused by an Armenian-type no credit economy, and the battered Soviet Zil cars. However, the roads were better than Yerevan's and there were numerous trappings of the Western world.

The official supporters meeting point was a Scottish pub in the town centre which simplistically was brilliant for no other reason that it played Big Country, Skids and The Proclaimers. I grew up listening to Stuart Adamson's music and for me The Skids were close to that ultimate in late 70s punk crap in Sham 69, which drove my Dad mad, as I listened to 'Hersham Boys' and the like.

However, Drew warned us not to be too over the top, should we decide to flirt with the local talent. He suggested the local beauties, and beautiful they were, wore their leather micro belts and cropped tops for the benefit of their Azeri male masters and any 'booze goggled' drunken approach might lead to more than the sore head courtesy of too much alcohol.

Talking of which, some supporters actually went to this game just to sleep!

The Northern Ireland supporters were camped out in a part of the ground behind a corner flag, with vast swathes of open seating, allowing the needy amongst us to lie prostrate and comatose during the game. And how much did the trip cost!

That said, they didn't miss much though as the game always had a 0-0 written all over it. Northern Ireland were without the suspended Healy and Hughes, and Capaldi was absent with a broken leg. Whilst the team had their chances there was never a glaring miss and few could complain about the result.

The flight home was early on Sunday, complete with the team, who needed to return to base to prepare for Austria on Wednesday, whilst I needed to return to get two days of work in, still being short of holidays following the Caribbean sojourn.

Of course, Easyjet were the preferred carrier, but the trip actually began the previous afternoon on a Hackney bound bus, as BBC Radio Ulster were on the phone looking for an interview. This actually occurred in the car on the way to the airport at around 6.30 a.m., and was apparently repeated at 8.00 a.m. I think this is the right place to apologise to those whose cornflakes went stale and milk tasted sour as they woke to my harsh Lancastrian tones! Personally, I wasn't scared, I was crapping myself!

On single day holidays like this, I think it important to try, sometimes not very hard, to do something constructive, which often means playing golf. We tried, but the autumnal elements caught up with us, and the pre-match hype took over, particularly as the team party were staying in the accompanying golf course hotel.

There was still a feeling of post-Cardiff optimism amongst Roy, Dessie and Gavin and the match itself was the exact opposite to the Azerbaijan affair. In short, Northern Ireland 2-3 down equalised, thanks to Stuart Elliott, with the last kick off the game, thereby creating what I feel was a sea change in team psychology.

Northern Ireland no longer appeared to lie down and accept their fate, as was the case in previous regimes. Instead they threw caution to the wind going all out to equalise, inclusive of goalkeeper Maik Taylor in the opposition penalty area, and deservedly got their reward. Under the previous regimes over these nine years, I cannot remember Northern Ireland coming back from behind, save once in Copenhagen, yet Sanchez' team had done it twice. Once in Barbados and now in a competitive game, and as David Currie pointed out, it lifted us a place in the qualifying group to the dizzy heights of fourth, as international football went into winter hibernation.

Lawrie Sanchez had brought us a goal, a win, and some bottle, and as the aura of an England game was on the horizon the chance to test the team against one of the world's best.

In November, I had a rather more personal test, which thankfully revealed I was cancer free, as a water based cyst in the form of an epydidymus was diagnosed. It was bizarre in some respects, for as I left Luton and Dunstable hospital, I just had nothing to worry about. Literally nothing, and though this was a peculiarly empty feeling, it was also a bloody good one, with the moral being, 'Guys! Check your balls', and not the lottery ones on a Saturday night!

FOR 2005, READ 2002, AND 2003

The test run for Old Trafford in March was against Canada in Belfast in February. Hardly a glamour fixture, but one which filled Windsor Park, as I just hoped the game was better than the 1999 affair. It wasn't, as the team succumbed to a ten man Canada team who had one meaningful attempt on goal all night. This precision point bullet header into Maik Taylor's net was clinical, yes, but also a disaster for everyone's moral, although the major talk always was of England, except in Windsor Avenue.

In the IFA's offices talk was of Lesley, who had given birth that morning to a baby boy, latterly named Ben. Karen Butler, who has the dubious privilege of arranging seating and ticketing at Windsor Park, gave me the news, which was a personal relief, as I knew Lesley was worried about things as her (early) expectant date had passed by. One of the great things about Lesley is trust, in that you could give her a £20 note and ask for it back in a year's time knowing that she would give you the same one. Things like that are important to me and probably why we have developed our friendship over the years.

In March, the mobile was constantly ringing with acquaintances asking what my plans were for the England game, as uniquely Northern Ireland were coming to me along with some 10,000 supporters, but only 6,700 tickets. This caused a number of upset travel plans, but Howard Wells, the new IFA chief executive headed off a potential PR disaster by arranging a big screen at City of Manchester Stadium.

Imagine the simple scenario. 6,700 supporters inside a ground, all in green watching Northern Ireland, outsinging the 60,000 'home' supporters and beating the English aristocrats? Well some of it was true, save the result as Northern Ireland succumbed 0-4. However, for the first 45 minutes, the team somehow kept a (charmed) blank sheet and I was beginning to wonder! We did not look as if we were going to score as David Healy cut an impossible furrow, trying to latch onto occasional long balls before Rio Ferdinand and John Terry snuffed him out, but could we just hold on for a draw. This would make my £20,000 plus outlay on watching Northern Ireland somehow justifiable in my mind as my half time fantasies ran amok. Sadly it wasn't to be, as two early second half goals caught the team cold and enforced a harsh reality check, until the following September that was, when every supporter's fantasy was realized, as Northern Ireland actually beat England 1-0.

The support once sang, 'W'ere gonna win 5-4' (in our dreams) to the Old Trafford church and sums up the attitude of the support on this occasion. It was an entertaining day out, even for Marty, who had flown in from Iraq for the occasion, and could not be construed as much else. The reality is that 99% of the time, Northern Ireland cannot compete with such class and need to cut their cloth against the lesser nations, and try to be the best of the second or third tier.

One such nation in that bracket is Poland and Northern Ireland certainly created a lot of nuisance value four days later in Warsaw.

This fixture began the second half of the qualifying series and from the team's point of view, they were far better than seven months previously. No silly early concessions, six corners in the first half, a James Quinn snapshot from 25 yards, and goalkeeper Maik Taylor inspired in the goal, continuing his form from Saturday and the older amongst us likening him to Pat Jennings.

Though I cannot remember, Jennings saved Northern Ireland from some real pummelling's in the 70's and 80's and now Taylor was similarly associated, with one particular '1on1' save coming to mind in this game. However, heroics can't last interminably and the goal was breached three minutes from time. Worryingly though, Northern Ireland had not scored for three games now and echoes of the 'barren' years were becoming all too apparent, particularly with Germany visiting Windsor Park in June.

As for the support, some 700 made the trip: perhaps not surprising given it was Easter week with many making a long holiday after the England experience. 'Everybody' was on parade, including a recovering Corney and the usual sleeping suspects who are so paralytic even the deafening support does not stir them!

Touristy wise, I had not been to Poland for twelve years and grim facades were still in evidence in the suburbs, but as with most other ex-communist central seats, the city hub has been restored to an antique stature along with contemporary plate glass hotels and financial offices. From an outsider looking in, I find the metamorphosis of (near) Eastern Europe over the last fifteen years nothing short of incredible. Sure Western finance and associated conglomerates have been a major force, but the willingness of the people to adopt a once alien lifestyle must be congratulated. As for Poland, from Eastern Bloc to EU and NATO, communist to capitalist, control to destiny, and hopeless to optimistic, life must have been traumatic in the early 90s, but now it looks good from this snapshot visit, to such an extent I am looking to but a property in one of the new Eastern European tigers. Who knows, there was once a Calais supporters club, number of members, one. Maybe there could be a Warsaw or Tallinn club!

FULL CIRCLE: JUNE 2005

The evolution of a standardized football calendar necessitates numerous international 'weeks', one which takes place in early June. However, on this occasion, the 'home' nations had decided not take arrange Group 6 qualifiers, with England undertaking a brand-selling North American tour and Northern Ireland commencing their 125th anniversary celebrations with a prestige friendly against Germany.

Germany were not the international force they were of the 1990s and had suffered both from a dearth of natural talent and numerous embarrassing results (draws against Lithuania and Iceland and only a 2-1 victory against the Faeroe Islands in qualifying for Euro 2004), yet they somehow reached the final of the 2002 World Cup, and as 2006 World Cup hosts, were still considered a top-draw friendly opposition.

As World Cup hosts, the Germans were also hosts to the much maligned FIFA Confederations Cup in mid-June, which would provide the Germans which some much needed 'competitive' football.

Countries which entertain major finals are seen as being open to jeopardising their own progress in the competition because for at least two years prior to the event, the team can only play friendly fixtures, which in crude terms have no real meaning, and obviously lack a competitive edge. To negate this, the Germans had arranged some local 'derby' fixtures against Holland and arranged a team 'bonding' tour to the Far East, when the Bundesliga was in winter hibernation. The Confederations Cup, which continental champions (or whoever can replace them) play in, was therefore important, as at least it was competitive and a chance for the 'new' German team, under the tutelage of Jurgen Klinsmann, whose brief was to simply win the World Cup, to test their abilities.

Of course, the Germans needed the pre-tournament build-up and what could be considered an 'easy' fixture against Northern Ireland was in the offing.

The match itself was somewhat unique for Northern Ireland, in that as well as being a 'commemorative' fixture; it was due to be played on a Saturday evening, rather than at a functional 3 p.m.

Personally, in the days leading up to the game, I had feelings of worry, fear and personal pride. Worry that I had not missed a game for 9 years and 350 odd days and things could still go wrong with a cancelled flight or more importantly an errant match ticket, as there was genuine confusion over whether Harry Simpson or Clarke Gibson had said tickets. The fear was centred on the fact the proceeding Monday I was starting a new job and had the expected 'don't know what to expect' butterflies. However, both feelings were latterly overcome by personal pride, in that I had been to 77 consecutive matches over ten years. Some were simple and organised, such as the home fixtures, but many were a nightmare. Travelling through Romania twice to get to Moldova and the Caribbean experience immediately spring to mind, but at the head of the list was the trip to Finland in October 1999. Having to arrange a flight in a foreign country, depending on a train service I had never used and depending on Sarah Pollitt's sister to do the taxi driving in Paris was a nightmare, but I needn't have worried with hindsight, as all worked out in the end, but initially such 'planned' logistics can cause a few nightmares.

In the lead up to the game, I had found out that Rebecca had been speaking to David Currie, but neither had been willing to discuss details, save Rebecca saying that something had been 'arranged'.

I often fantasise about being a football luminary and being able to access all areas of a match theatre, inclusive of shaking hands with the players on the pitch prior to the national anthems and have said that should I win the lottery, I would pay the fee for Brazil to play at Windsor Park, but demand I was a dignitary, shook hands with the players, had my friends sit in the directors box, and I would play the last ten minutes of the fixture! Even Jimmy Saville could not fix that, but dreaming is free!

Could something like this occur, I was thinking, no hoping, to celebrate ten years. No such luck, but a spread in the match programme was the 'arrangement'. It was a great surprise, but the photo of my wearing an Armenian policeman's helmet, I had borrowed for a photo-call, did not do my modelling career justice!

To commemorate the game, and to create some valuable football community based funding, Umbro and the IFA had produced a new strip which was to replicate a historical strip (cost £35), as well as having a pre-game roll of honour at Windsor Park, in what was a kind of early summer party atmosphere, I feel is (as mentioned) created when fans are peculiarly coatless.

For 60 seconds in the game the atmosphere became euphoric, as David Healy converted a 15th minute penalty following a hand ball. 1-0 to Northern Ireland, but could it last? No way, as Germany equalised within seconds and the visitors, by now down to ten men, gradually took over, with Michael Ballack pulling the team strings in midfield, outstanding. It was obvious Klinsmann was building a team around this guy who effortlessly strode around the pitch, creating brilliant passing and running angles, which was a joy to watch. The result, bearing in mind the circumstances, was perhaps not particularly important, as the IFA was 125, with England, Wales, Portugal and possibly Italy to visit Belfast, and I was 10. I had done it, and whilst not intentionally intending to take this journey back in 1995, after the Latvian debacle, it's been a great, if not a cheap, trip.

EPILOGUE

The grey Major years, The Spice Girls, the Blair evolution, the loss to Albania, the losses to Armenia, the twin towers attacks, Muslim terrorism et al all came and came (or went) in the last ten years. It's been a great trip, but what of the future.

Blair is still in Downing Street, leading us to a luvvy-duvvy European super state, apparently the world is getter hotter, and Bin Laden is still sticking two fingers up at the US, but what of the future on the football pitch?

Yes, I'd like to say Northern Ireland will qualify for a major final and beat the leading playing nations, but the England affair in Old Trafford brings in the cold reality that this will likely not occur, unless luck takes an extraordinary turn. As intimated though, there is no reason why the team should not evolve as being the best of the rest, with nuisance value against the Ukraine's and Romania's of this world whilst looking at regularly beating the Switzerland's and even the Scotland's. In the short term a more potent strike force could render this possible, but the reality is a twenty goal a season man of world class quality to compliment Healy and Quinn is not on the horizon. True, Stuart Elliott and Stephen Jones often netted for Hull and Crewe in 2004 and 2005, but against Italy or Holland?

In my view, Northern Ireland is a small country and theoretically should not be eating at the top table, but three clichés do spring to mind. 'It's a funny old game', 'It only takes a second to score a goal.', and who knows 'The best things can come to those who wait"! Just ask David Healy and any of the 11,000 faithful who were at Windsor Park on 7th September, 2005!